Circulating Fear

Circulating Fear

Japanese Horror, Fractured Realities, and New Media

Lindsay Nelson

LEXINGTON BOOKS
Lanham • Boulder • New York • London

Published by Lexington Books
An imprint of The Rowman & Littlefield Publishing Group, Inc.
4501 Forbes Boulevard, Suite 200, Lanham, Maryland 20706
www.rowman.com

86-90 Paul Street, London EC2A 4NE, United Kingdom

Copyright © 2021 by The Rowman & Littlefield Publishing Group, Inc.

A different version of chapter two, "Choosing Illusion: Mediated Reality and the Spectacle of the Idol in Kōji Shiraishi's *Shirome*," appeared in *Journal of Japanese and Korean Cinema*, 8:2, 2016, pp. 140-155.

All rights reserved. No part of this book may be reproduced in any form or by any electronic or mechanical means, including information storage and retrieval systems, without written permission from the publisher, except by a reviewer who may quote passages in a review.

British Library Cataloguing in Publication Information Available

Library of Congress Cataloging-in-Publication Data Available

ISBN 9781793613677 (cloth: alk. paper) | ISBN 9781793613691 (paperback) | ISBN 9781793613684 (electronic)

Contents

List of Figures	vii
Acknowledgments	ix
Introduction	1
1 Circulating Urban Legends: From 2channel to *Toshimaen: The Movie*	25
2 Idols, Japanese Horror, and Fractured Realities: *Shirome*	49
3 The Haunted Forest: Circulating Aokigahara	71
4 From *Ringu* to *Rings*: Porous Screens and Virtual Windows in the Later *Ringu* Films	91
Conclusion: Living in Virtual Windows	111
Bibliography	117
Index	131
About the Author	135

List of Figures

Figure 0.1	Bubble tea advertisement featuring Sadako	2
Figure 1.1	Watching *2channel Curse* on a laptop	38
Figure 1.2	Multiple windows and frames in *Webcam Call* (Nagae Jirō 2010)	39
Figure 1.3	Comments scroll chaotically across the screen of a Niconico video in *Toshimaen: The Movie* (Takahashi Hiroshi 2019)	43
Figure 2.1	"Eguchi Aimi" appears in a Glico commercial	55
Figure 2.2	The members of Momoiro Clover Z confess their "true feelings" to the camera in *Shirome* (Shiraishi Kōji 2010)	64
Figure 3.1	The "Akkīna" character in the film *Suicide Forest Village* (Shimizu Takashi 2021)	78
Figure 3.2	The "Akkīna" character in a video promoting the scenic beauty of Aokigahara	79
Figure 4.1	A man's face is reflected in his computer screen as he watches a live video broadcast in *Sadako 3D* (Hanabusa Tsutomu 2012)	102
Figure 4.2	The computer screen is reflected in Mayu's eyes as she watches her brother's video in *Sadako* (Nakata Hideo 2019)	107

Acknowledgments

No book project happens in a vacuum, and in the fifteen years since I began my graduate studies countless people have been there to nurture, to offer practical advice, to read drafts, and simply to share a cup of tea and commiseration when things didn't go as planned.

I began my graduate studies at Tokyo's Sophia University in 2006, in what was then the Department of Comparative Culture. Angela Yiu not only introduced me to Japanese literature and film, but also provided all kinds of helpful advice when it came to applying to PhD programs in the United States. I still look to her classes when I create syllabi for my own.

During my PhD studies at the University of Southern California, Anne McKnight was dissertation chair, mentor, and teacher—someone whose classes and body of work provided another model for the kind of academic I wanted to become. Years later, she would also help me with this book's prospectus and offer all kinds of nuts-and-bolts advice about publishing and navigating the academic job market. I owe her a lot. Akira Lippit's seminar on contemporary Japanese cinema introduced me to Japanese horror films and helped me craft the essays that would become my dissertation, and his work has been hugely helpful in informing my own thinking about Japanese cinema as a whole. Huge gratitude to the other members of my dissertation committee, David Bialock and Roberto Diaz.

I would not have survived grad school without the wonderful friends and colleagues who helped me make sense of it all, offered me a place to stay when I needed it, and just shared laughs and tears over good food on a regular basis: Sam Solomon, Colin Dickey, Nicole Antebi, Emilie Garrigou-Kempton, Alex Kempton, Seth Michelson, Vicki Conti, Sandra So Hee Chi Kim, Naomi Bergeron, Feng-Mei Heberer, Caterina Crisci, Michelle Har Kim, Garren Chew, Justin Tyler Clark, and Mary Traester, among many others. If I ever wrote anything meaningful during that time, it was because I was so determined to be as good as they were. Shaoling Ma is the best roommate, friend, and seminar classmate anyone could have asked for.

Ana Paulina Lee, Anne McKnight, and Miri Nakamura all read early drafts of my book prospectus and offered invaluable insights. Miri, Colleen Laird, and Raechel Dumas made comments on the first and second book drafts that helped shape it into something much more coherent—what's good here is very much thanks to them, and what isn't is my responsibility. Colleen in particular gave me such detailed and helpful comments on a later draft that helped all the pieces of the book finally begin to cohere.

In Tokyo, I was lucky to have a group of friends and colleagues to share tea, consultations, and writing dates with in local cafes. Thank you so much to Grace En-Yi Ting, Alexandra Hambleton, Laura Clark, Saeki Eiko, Lucy Glasspool, Naomi Berman, Rachel Walzer, Shibata Yuki, Kristi Govella, and Jordan Wyndelts for chats and late-night text exchanges. Thank you to Aaron Gerow, Alexander Zahlten, and Christophe Thouny for advice, support, workshop hosting, and generally keeping me in the loop about all things Japanese film. Thank you to Miranda Larsen and Katarzyna Ancuta for their wealth of knowledge about contemporary horror movies and trends.

The Japan Foundation generously supported a year of dissertation research from 2010 to 2011 and is one of the reasons I am (happily) still in Tokyo today. The staff at the Japan Foundation Library were incredibly generous with their time whenever I needed help accessing particular books and articles. Yoshihara Yukari was a wonderful mentor during my fellowship and continues to be a friend and a valuable source of advice and scholarship. At the University of Tokyo, Yaguchi Yujin and Itatsu Yuko were excellent faculty mentors who did far more than their fair share of service. At Meiji University, my friend and colleague Ishiyama Noriko helped with Japanese translations. Johnny George, Toraiwa Naoko, and Hirobe Izumi were the best *sempai* to have in navigating the ins and outs of Japanese university life.

Thank you to Nicolette Amstutz for first approaching me about publishing with Lexington, and thank you to Jessica Tepper for helping me navigate every step of the publication process with patience and understanding. Thank you to everyone at Lexington who did the work of proofing, formatting, and promoting the book. Thank you to Christopher Lehrich for proofreading and to Lori Morimoto for creating the index.

My students at Meiji University and Tokyo University have taught me just as much as I've taught them, and I'm grateful for their frequent insights into the worlds of Japanese popular culture, social media, and the everyday lives of young people.

To my wonderful in-laws in Brazil, thank you for welcoming me so warmly into the family. To my extended family: my aunt Cynthia Nelson, uncles John and Dan Nelson, cousins Travis and Ryan Nelson, half-brothers Luke and David Allen Nelson, my step-siblings Adrienne Sneed, Dylan Sneed, and Bethany Blankenship—thank you for making my world a bigger and better place to grow up in.

To my sister Lesley, thank you for the late-night chats and text exchanges that kept me grounded.

To my parents, without whom none of this would have been possible: my mother Debbie Sneed, my father David Nelson, my stepmother Jennifer Nelson, and my stepfather Dennis Sneed. Mom and Dad, thank you for making me feel that I could do anything and being supportive while I was on the very winding road that got me to where I am now.

Last but never least, to my partner, Rafael Caetano dos Santos, my light in dark places. Thank you for watching all those scary movies with me, telling me I was good at things when I was convinced that I wasn't, and cheering me up with cat videos when I needed it. This book is for you.

Introduction

In May 2019, Japan's bubble tea craze had not yet reached a fever pitch, but advertisements and small shops were starting to appear all over Tokyo. One of these ads, displayed on a large placard outside of a Wendy's/First Kitchen, featured an image of a greenish mint chocolate milk tea, black pearls of tapioca floating on top, and dark ribbons of chocolate drizzling down the sides. Looking closer, one might notice a sketch of a body climbing out of a screen, long hair obscuring its face. This was Sadako, the ghostly, malevolent spirt at the center of multiple books and films in the *Ring* (*Ringu*)[1] franchise. The ad, with the tagline "This deliciousness is ruthless" (*Kono oishisa, yōshanai*),[2] was a promotional tie-in for the latest offering in the franchise, *Sadako* (dir. Nakata Hideo[3] 2019). Examining this photo of the advertisement even more closely, other details emerge. The black-and-white sketch of Sadako's body climbing out of a screen, simple as it may be, is immediately recognizable. There is the fact that the entire composite image—tea, film poster, cartoon, and ad copy—is positioned on a large placard that identifies it as a piece of advertising. And then there is the fact that I was able to easily take a photo of this placard, positioned outside a restaurant in the "real" world, on my own smartphone, via which I could then easily upload and share the image to multiple social media platforms. Long since deleted from my phone, it probably still exists in multiple spaces online, and will for a long time to come. Like her famous curse, Sadako lingers in many forms (figure 0.1).

This certainly was not the first instance of cross-marketing for a Japanese horror film, or even the first caricature of Sadako, the dark presence who kills her victims with the wrath of a single, staring eye that peeks out from under a mane of long black hair. In the late 2010s in Japan one could also purchase Sadako "stickers" on the popular LINE chat app, which featured Sadako making heart signs with her hands and crawling out of a well with

Figure 0.1 Bubble tea advertisement featuring Sadako. *Source*: Photo taken by author.

"good morning" (*ohayō*) written in text next to her image. Around the time of the release of the sequel/spinoff *Sadako vs. Kayako* (dir. Shiraishi Kōji 2016), a series of theater advertisements used Sadako and Kayako (the evil entity at the center of the *The Grudge* [*Ju-on*] film and TV franchise) to sell popcorn and lecture audiences about good theater manners. Photographs of Kayako and Toshio, her pale-faced, ghostly son, were featured on Instagram, where they stared mournfully at the camera while doing everyday things like picnicking under cherry blossoms and doing laundry. The year 2019 also saw the release of Koma Natsumi's manga *Sadako at the End of the World* (*Shūmatsu no Sadako-san*), which imagined Sadako as a kind of cuddly (but still murderous) friend to two young girls in a postapocalyptic landscape.

The many incarnations of Sadako, Kayako, and Toshio, circulated via films, YouTube videos, print and digital advertisements, Instagram, and Twitter, reveal the extent to which Japanese horror narratives, characters, and images have spread across a variety of literal and figurative frames. No longer relegated to films and TV programs, these small pieces of the larger Japanese horror film world are now present on social media, as "mind your manners" advertising in Japanese movie theaters, in music videos for their films' song tie-ins, and in walk-through attractions at Japanese amusement parks. The sharing of these many small pieces of a larger story calls to mind Azuma Hiroki's theory of "database consumption," which argues that, rather than "grand narratives," *otaku* and other fans of manga and anime are now much more focused on smaller, component pieces of stories, or "small narratives" (Azuma 2009, 54). In the case of Japanese horror, these pieces of a larger narrative move between different types of screens and universes, easily consumed and shared. Japanese horror characters and images have been shared, satirized, and re-imagined, importantly, as new media objects[4] which, like Sadako's endlessly replicating video cassette, "can exist in different, potentially infinite versions" (Manovich 2001, 36). Platforms such as Twitter, Instagram, YouTube, and Niconico (a Japanese video-sharing site similar to YouTube) now play a part not only in the marketing of Japanese horror films but also in how audience perceptions of their characters, motifs, and paratexts[5] are shaped. And within Japanese horror films, a focus on the "ghostliness" (and dangers) of smart phones, video streaming services, and digital media technology has gradually supplanted the genre's previous focus on cell phones, video cassettes, floppy disks, and TV sets. These films constantly shift between different types of screens, showing us characters watching live video broadcasts on computers or smartphones, characters filming each other on handheld cameras or smartphones, and even images of our own reflections in screens, if we happen to be watching (as many of us do) on our own home computers, smartphones, or tablets. Just as Sadako frequently breaks through physical screens to attack her victims, Japanese horror films also present us with shifting barriers and boundaries via the screens and conceptual/visual frames that surround these stories.

On a narrative level, Japanese horror films have always been deeply concerned with certain kinds of media objects/technologies and their potential dangers, from the cursed video cassette of *Ringu* to the haunted Internet of *Pulse* (*Kairo*, dir. Kurosawa Kiyoshi 2001) to the cursed cell phones of *One Missed Call* (*Chakushin ari*, dir. Miike Takashi 2003). Maekawa (2015) notes that J-horror[6] has frequently been referred to as "media horror" for its depiction of curses that are transmitted through the screens of televisions, computers, and cell phones (Maekawa 2015, 12). J-horror films as media horror "participate in the project of global modernity" in the way that they focus on "anxieties brought to bourgeois everyday life" by new technologies (Kinoshita 2009, 111). Kristen Lacefield has examined the "media anxiety" that the *Ringu* films produced, particularly in their explicit connections between death and photography, given that those who watch Sadako's cursed video are pictured in their final moments as a film negative, "literally negated, turned into negatives" (Lacefield 2010, 10). This narrative focus on media technology and devices has also frequently been connected to the manner of Japanese horror films' dissemination—Carlos Rojas (2014) notes that U.S. director Gore Verbinski first saw the Japanese version of *Ringu* on a very low-quality video tape, and promotion of the English-language remake *The Ring* included placing unlabeled promotional tapes in certain locations around the country, accompanied by "a suggestive note saying something to the effect of 'watch this and die'" (Rojas 2014, 435). Mitsuyo Wada-Marciano argues that it is important to examine the "materiality" of Japanese horror films, given that J-horror's "affinity with the DVD format" has allowed J-horror to "[extend] its reach through an enormous amount of works and thereby (broaden) its categorical parameters" (Wada-Marciano 2012, 46). In defining J-horror as a genre, Maekawa also argues that a starting point in video production rather than film (*firumu*) is a defining characteristic of J-horror—early efforts were low-budget and produced quickly, which also aided in widespread, speedy distribution (Maekawa 2012, 6). Thus, in their narrative focus, means of production, and means of dissemination, Japanese horror films raise questions about the importance of/anxiety surrounding certain media devices and media technologies.

How should we think about Japanese horror films and their relationship to media devices and technologies, then, in a time when social and digital media devices and technologies are omnipresent in the lives of large numbers of people? One important point to consider is that in the 2010s and beyond, the media landscape in which Japanese horror films are created and disseminated is even more saturated with information, screens, devices, and platforms than the media landscape of the early to mid-2000s. The stories told in Japanese horror films themselves are still frequently focused on media anxiety, but the fearful technology in question—social media, video streaming—is even more personal and interactive. It is also an important means through which these contemporary horror narratives are consumed, shaped, and disseminated. And with this contemporary mediated reality come new versions of perennial Japanese horror film concerns: namely, the question of what is real, the inherent ghostliness of different media devices and technologies, and the ways that different forms of media fracture and reshape reality for both characters and audiences. The ad copy for a 2020 Sadako-focused walk-through experience in Odaiba that mixes video and live actors illustrates this tension: it promises a terror that isn't "indirect" (*kansetsu-teki*) but one that feels like a "real experience" (*jittaiken*) (Joypolis 2020).

This book, then, is primarily concerned with these questions: how do Japanese horror films and their English-language remakes/offshoots from the 2010s and beyond use the trappings of realness (carefully mixed with obvious fictions) to create a sense of fear and discomfort? What role do media devices, platforms, and technologies such as smart phones, YouTube, social media, and video streaming play in both the narratives of Japanese horror films and in shaping our perception of them? How have new media devices and technologies changed the way that horror stories are told? Finally, looking beyond Japanese horror films themselves, how have certain images, ideas, and characters (the Aokigahara forest, Sadako) been circulated and reshaped via new media technologies, and how has that circulation and reshaping informed their depiction in film? In examining these questions, I make use of a theoretical framework that includes new media studies, cultural studies, and Japanese horror cinema studies.

Though my primary focus is Japanese horror films, my analysis expands beyond films and into YouTube videos, "haunted" spaces, English-language horror films that take place in Japan, online urban legends, and marketing/promotional campaigns for Japanese horror films, all of which I argue play a part both in the narratives depicted in Japanese horror films and in the way that those films are shaped and disseminated. I place these films and their accompanying paratexts in the context of changes in the new media landscape: the ubiquity of smart phones and social media, the ease of user remediation through platforms such as YouTube and Twitter, and the way that Japanese horror film narratives have shifted their focus from the dangers of TV and cell phones to the dangers of social media, YouTube, and smart phones. I also go beyond Japan to examine how certain "horrific" Japanese characters, spaces, and ideas are interpreted and reshaped in other countries, as well as how certain horror motifs (vengeful female spirits, young women in peril) are interpreted and reshaped within Japan. Ultimately, I argue that, by forcing viewers to constantly re-examine what they are seeing (and how they are seeing it) through the depiction of a variety of screens and new media objects, contemporary Japanese horror films present us with a fractured sense of reality and authenticity. Japanese horror films' sense of reality/authenticity is purposefully muddled through a narrative focus on new media technologies that are known for manipulating our sense of what is real and authentic, through the use of many literal and figurative frames-within-frames, and through the mixing of visual, auditory, and narrative cues that mix fiction and nonfiction.

THE EVOLUTION OF JAPANESE HORROR FILMS

I define Japanese horror films as films that deal with ghosts, the supernatural, monsters, and haunting, or simply films that exist primarily to frighten or unsettle. When one speaks of "J-horror," though, the term usually calls to mind a small group of films released from the late 1990s to the early 2000s, frequently featuring vengeful female ghosts, some sort of malevolent force that moves via TVs, phones, or the Internet, and an emphasis on atmospheric dread rather than jump-scares or gore. Representative films include *Ringu*, *The Grudge* (*Ju-on*, dir. Shimizu Takashi 2002) and their many sequels and prequels, as well as Kurosawa Kiyoshi's *Cure* (*Kyua*, 1997) and *Pulse*. Given that several of the directors, screenwriters, and producers of J-horror often worked together and were also avid cinephiles who published works of film scholarship, Kinoshita argues that J-horror can be viewed as a "movement" and a "discourse" (Kinoshita 2009, 104–106). It was a "homosocial film community" of men who worked together and frequently commented on each other's films (Kinoshita 2021). Key figures included directors Nakata Hideo, Shimizu Takashi, and Kurosawa Kiyoshi, screenwriters Takahashi Hiroshi and Konaka Chiaki, and producer Ichise Takashige (Kinoshita 2009, 105). Many of the key figures of the movement remain active today—in addition to sequels to the original *Ringu* films, Nakata has directed *Stigmatized Properties* (*Jiko bukken: Kowai madori*, 2020), while Shimizu has created a "scary village" trilogy that includes *Suicide Forest Village* (*Jukai mura*, 2021, discussed in chapter 3). Kurosawa is perhaps better known in the 2010s and 2020s for dramas like the award-winning *Wife of a Spy* (*Supai no tsuma*, 2020), but he also continues to make horror films like *Creepy* (*Kurīpī*, 2016).

Mitsuyo Wada-Marciano not only shares Kinoshita's view of J-horror as a movement but also sees it as "a particular body of films: that is, a genre," arguing that the movement "is not limited to Japan and is rather more permeable and interconnected with other areas—namely Asia or, in a sense, even the United States via Hollywood remakes" (Wada-Marciano 2012, 29). Though J-horror was often marketed abroad as quintessentially "Japanese," Takahashi Hiroshi argues that Japanese films owe more to English-language films like *The Haunting* than to specifically "Japanese" folk tales or horror sensibilities (Brown 2018, 3–4). In 2005, Christopher Sharrett also noted that part of the appeal of J-horror for U.S. audiences was that the films featured "a relationship to society similar to that of American horror in the post-Vietnam

1970s," markedly different from the "high-tech roller coaster rides" that U.S. horror films had become (Sharrett 2005, xii). Brown, building on Takahashi, argues that J-horror "has been characterized by transnational hybridity from its very inception . . . global microflows have cross-fertilized Japanese horror and greatly complexified how one situates the 'J' in 'J-horror'" (Brown 2018, 6), while Elisabeth Scherer (2016) argues that the female ghosts that appear so frequently in Japanese horror films are "nomadic entities open to transformation and transnational cooperation" (62). For Yomota Inuhiko, Japanese cinema as a whole has long been characterized by "an overwhelming cultural hybridity—the will to build an entirely new composite form by layering heterogeneous cultural sources" (Yomota 2019, 16). Even if certain images and motifs from J-horror—ghostly girls with long black hair, for example—may be perceived by some as "Japanese," the films, like so many Japanese films, are in fact the result of many different cinematic and cultural influences.

Wada-Marciano also notes J-horror's connection to new media technologies, arguing that in the "post-studio period" of the late 1990s and 2000s, many filmmakers were "quick to embrace new media, whether digital video or computer editing, in order to trim their production budgets and schedules" (Wada-Marciano 2012, 32). Building on Wada-Marciano, Maekawa (2015) notes J-horror's frequent use of "frames within frames," arguing that a further frame "layer" exists in J-horror's origins in video, and in the way that it was circulated via information in young people's phones, online reviews, and rental videos (12). For Maekawa, "the medium frame exists inside and outside of the movie frame" (Maekawa 2015, 12). In its manner of distribution and consumption, J-horror also "(uses) the rhetoric of new media, and in the dialectic relationship between film and new media, the genre takes on the role of a storyteller appealing to younger audiences who are already steeped in a variety of digital technologies, including computer games, DVDs, and home theater systems" (Wada-Marciano 2012, 35). As we will see, when it comes to Japanese horror films produced in the 2010s and beyond, this relationship to new media becomes even more complex and layered, as film narratives become more focused on social media, streaming, and smartphones. In these films, a tension often exists between newer media objects and devices (often in the form of streaming, digital videos, and smartphones) and "old" media (often in the form of photographs and video cassettes). "Old" media is more likely to be imbued with nostalgia, while newer media is regarded with suspicion.

The aesthetic, characters, and settings that characterized J-horror's distinctive style developed in the 1990s partly out of a desire to produce cheap films that relied less on dramatic visual effects or gory violence than on atmospheric "true stories" of hauntings and strange occurrences. Interestingly, as

Alexander Zahlten notes, the focus on atmosphere over violence was arguably a response to the infamous murders committed by Miyazaki Tsutomu, the so-called "*otaku* killer" who murdered four young girls between 1988 and 1989. Because of media reports about Miyazaki's large collection of manga, the murders set off a moral panic that connected *otaku* with violence and deviant behavior. During this time "video companies were forced to retreat from the production and distribution of explicitly bloody horror films . . . companies were searching for a way to return to the horror film market when Tsuruta Norio, who was working as a subtitle producer for JHV, proposed a series focusing on atmospheric, supernatural horror centered on schoolgirls having scary experiences" (Zahlten 2017, 162–163). As Zahlten and Brown have noted, the J-horror aesthetic owes much to the *True Scary Stories* (*Hontō ni atta kowai hanashi*) series produced by Tsuruta Norio beginning in the early 1990s, a series of short episodes based on urban legends made quickly and cheaply for TV (Zahlten 2017, 163; Brown 2018, 2). Producer Takahashi Hiroshi and director Nakata Hideo, who both worked on *True Scary Stories*, borrowed heavily from its aesthetic when they created *Ringu*, arguably the first major J-horror hit, which would go on to enjoy international popularity and inspire many imitations (Zahlten 2017, 163).

Though J-horror was at least partially born out of a desire to *distance* the film industry from real-world violence, the genre frequently engaged with Japanese social problems such as suicide, social isolation, and the breakdown of family/social support networks. *Dark Water* (*Honogurai mizu no soko kara,* dir. Nakata Hideo 2002) focused on the struggles of single motherhood and the consequences of parental neglect; *Pulse* dealt with loneliness and isolation specific to young people living in urban areas; *One Missed Call* and *The Locker* (*Shibuya Kaidan*, dir. Horie Kei 2004) both dealt with child abuse and child abandonment. Many J-horror films presented two levels of horror: the horror of vengeful spirits or monsters and the horror of everyday life for people who had fallen through the cracks of Japan's (weakening) social safety nets.

Depictions of murder or tragic death in horror films occasionally coincided with real-world tragedies. Director and film scholar Kurosawa Kiyoshi wrote that his landmark 1997 horror film *Cure*, about a man who seems to be able to compel others to commit murder through hypnosis, was released at around the same time as the Kobe child murders, in which a fourteen-year-old boy murdered two younger children and left the severed head of one of his victims in front of a school gate (Kurosawa 2001a, 12). Kurosawa wrote that audiences seemed frustrated that his film was both "too real" and "not real enough"—in light of the graphic details surrounding the child murders and the sarin gas attack by a doomsday cult in Tokyo two years before, Kurosawa felt that audiences had perhaps expected a more "documentary-like" exploration of a killer (Kurosawa 2001a, 12). This mix of a "documentary-like" aesthetic (seen in found-footage-style camera work or simply films that appear to be low-budget) and fictional horror stories, as well as a mixing of supernatural and "everyday" horror, continues to be a feature of Japanese horror films in the 2010s and beyond. *Innocent Curse* (*Kodomo tsukai*, dir. Shimizu Takashi 2017) focused on child abuse and pedophilia, *Creepy* vividly broke down questions about familial and neighborly relationships, and the vengeful spirit character of *Toshimaen: The Movie* (*Eiga: Toshimaen*, dir. Takahashi Hiroshi,[7] 2019, discussed in chapter 1) is a victim of school bullying. Now, however, the tension between reality and fiction, and the frequent uncertainty about where one ends and the other begins, is further "fractured" by these films' frequent connections to social media and the illusions of intimacy and authenticity that those platforms and technologies create.

Feelings of uncertainty surrounding communication technology in Japanese horror films have frequently been illustrated via images and stories of circuits, loops, and endless replication. Kurosawa Kiyoshi's film *Kairo* is usually translated as *Pulse*, but the title is actually closer to "circuit," perhaps indicating the film's conduit between the world of ghosts and the human world that seems to have taken hold via the Internet. Throughout the film, we hear the ominous (and now dated) sound of a dial-up modem trying to make a connection, establishing a pathway that will convert and transmit data back and forth from one place to another in a loop. In the case of the film, what emerges from the circuit are digital ghosts that exist somewhere between material and immaterial, human and specter—when one character tries to save himself from madness by grabbing one of the ghosts to prove that it's not "real," his hands close on a tangible body, even if the image of the ghost remains unclear. "But people don't really connect, you know," says another character of the Internet (Kurosawa 2001b). Data moves back and forth in an endless loop, but humans remain isolated. Sadako's cursed video spreads when others make physical copies of it (and in later sequels, when it is uploaded to video-sharing sites and shared via smart phones and computers). The *Tomie* series imagines a demonic presence who is born again and again in the body of a young woman. As discussed previously, these were also films that had an "affinity with the DVD format" (Wada-Marciano 2012, 46) and, in the case of *Ringu*, initially spread around the world via poorly made bootleg copies. The endless loops and circles continue today in an environment where sharing, copying, and remediation are easier than ever.

At the peak of their popularity, English-language versions of Japanese horror films including *Ringu*, *The Grudge*, *Pulse*, and *One Missed Call* were produced in the U.S. Repetition, but not exact copies. Citing Deleuze on Nietzschean repetition (the idea that "repetition is not the representation of an original, but the repetition of difference without an origin"), Aaron Gerow wonders whether horror is "the true genre of repetition" (Gerow 2002, 21). Given that "simulacra are the denial of the principle of identity (A=A), we can speculate whether it is not horror, often populated with figures who seem to be themselves yet are somehow not themselves . . . that persistently explores the opposite of identity (A=not A)" (Gerow 2002, 21). For Maekawa, the core (*kakushin*) of J-horror lies in the cross-referencing (*sōgo sanshō*) of fragments without origin, given that J-horror texts frequently have "no original text," only "multiple variations" which constantly "reference and dereference each other" in a way that "disrupts temporal order" (Maekawa 2015, 16–17). A lack of clear origin seems even more relevant when dealing with new media objects that blur the distinction between original and copy, or for which a definite origin is difficult to find.

Raechel Dumas sees simulacra and repetitions not necessarily as a source of horror, but as a way to break through barriers. Though not arguing that stories like *Ringu* are inherently feminist, she builds on Deleuze and Guattari's concepts of repetition, difference, and the simulacrum to argue that "an alternative framework might open up *Ring* to a subtly but importantly different reading, and one that creates space for understanding its simulacratic specter not as a confirmation of non-identity, but rather as an attempt to grapple with the possibility of a postmodern ontology that is grounded in the rise of the technological" (Dumas 2018, 49). An endlessly multiplying *shōjo* (young girl) could be seen, she argues, as a form of "resistance" against hegemonic narratives that often leave out certain subjectivities (40).[8] In my own 2012 PhD dissertation, I referred to Sadako as

> [a kind of] tech-womb . . . a thing born of her own rage and the physical technology of the video cassette and the dubbing machine, [who] gives birth not only to a fictional cycle of rage-infection, but to an entirely new way of spreading a film and a story throughout the world, through the fusion of a compelling story, the ingenuity of the viewers, and available technology that circumvents traditional methods of film distribution. (Nelson 2012, 120–121)

While repetition, as Gerow points out, is not unique to the Japanese horror genre or even horror as a whole, the motifs of circularity, doubling, rebirth, copying, and simulacra are present in many Japanese horror films from the early 2000s, and continue to feature in horror films from the 2010s and beyond.

How do these circuits, loops, and simulacra function in Japanese horror films made from the mid-2000s to the 2010s, when new media technologies and devices became central to both horror narratives and the way that those narratives were shaped and disseminated? I would argue that the circle/circuit/loop moves even faster and spreads over a much wider area now, as still images, videos, and text are passed from person to person and device to device across multiple platforms and countries. In titling this manuscript *Circulating Fear*, I refer to the way that frightening images from Japan (the Aokigahara forest, the young girl in peril, later incarnations of Sadako) are circulated at high speeds via films seen in theaters, DVDs, video streaming services, and social media platforms. As these images and fragments circulate between different screens, devices, and platforms, they are copied and reshaped—made into memes, used for personal profit, or co-opted to further Orientalist narratives (as with images of Aokigahara used in English-language media, discussed in chapter 3). What is circulated are not only an ever-shifting series of images and fragments, but also the sense of "fractured reality" that their accompanying horror films perpetuate. As I hope that this manuscript's chapters will illustrate, this fractured reality is visible in a variety of horror-focused texts that are connected to new media technologies and devices.

The success of J-horror both at home and abroad led to a great deal of academic analysis in the 2000s and early 2010s, much of which focused on these visual motifs of repetition/copying, as well as the theme of "media contagion" in films like *Ringu* (Rojas 2014; Stringer 2007). Sometimes circuits and loops were connected to Deleuzean notions of repetition and simulacra (Gerow 2002), as well as to ideas of order and chaos in relation to technology (Ancuta 2007). There was also a focus on the connection between characters/narratives of J-horror and real-world Japanese social problems (suicide, child abuse, and neglect, urban loneliness) that were often depicted side by side with the ghostly elements (Goldberg 2004; McRoy 2005; Balmain 2008) and the idea that Japanese horror films reflected the bleak reality of late-capitalist societies in which "identity becomes a purchasable, ultimately disposable commodity" (Iles 2005). Loops, repetition, and Deleuzean notions of the simulacra continued to be useful modes for analysis in the 2010s and beyond (Brown 2018; Dumas 2018; Maekawa 2015), particularly with regard to the way that certain Japanese horror films (and sometimes their remakes) often deal with a tension between original and copy (Wee 2014). Present in almost all of these analyses is an examination of the role of technology in Japanese horror films, in particular the inherent ghostliness of devices like the VCR in *Ringu* and computers/the Internet in *Pulse*. Recent Japanese scholarship has also focused on Japanese horror films' inherent fascination with the nature of reality, particularly as that reality is presented to us (and manipulated) via devices like the camera and the TV (Maekawa 2015; Ōshima 2010).

J-horror peaked fairly quickly—by 2005, the genre/brand had already been declared "dead" by the likes of the popular *Midnight Eye* Japanese film website (Rucka 2005). The mostly unsuccessful imitation films produced over the next decade led Steven T. Brown to argue that the J-horror brand "was not simply in its final death throes—it was already dead, if not yet buried" (Brown 2018, 2). The Japanese film industry had also gone through significant changes during this time, continuing to focus on committee-produced films based on popular manga and anime franchises. In focusing on the "industrial genres" of pink film, Kadokawa Film, and V-cinema, Alexander Zahlten argues that it is helpful to think of Japanese "film" (really, the commercial film industry) "in terms of mediated, usually moving, images easily tied to various media-mix models" (Zahlten 2017, 21). James Hadfield referred to the 2010s in Japan as a decade of "closed country cinema," where the most successful films, like 2018's *Code Blue: The Movie* (*Kōdo burū: Dokutāheri kinkyū kyūmei*, based on a successful TV series) were "highly parochial, catering to local audiences with ruthless efficiency" (Hadfield 2019). Many successful commercial Japanese films are based on established TV or anime series with large fan bases,[9] leading to films that are endlessly recyclable and designed for reproducibility.

In this context, Japanese horror films in the 2010s and beyond have also changed, seeking out new platforms for distribution (a 2020 entry in the *Ju-on* franchise, *Ju-on: Origins* [dir. Miyake Shō] was distributed via Netflix, as was Shimizu Takashi's 2021 film *Homunculus* [*Homunkurusu*]) and focusing more on their alliance with other industries (pop music and the world of pop idols and *tarento*, for example). *Ringu* director Nakata Hideo and director Kurosawa Kiyoshi have both made films starring former AKB48 members (Shimazaki Haruka and Maeda Atsuko), while promotion for Takashi Shimizu's *Innocent Curse* (2017) leaned heavily on magazine interviews and glossy photo spreads of its two male leads, former Johnny's Jr. performer Takizawa Hideaki and Hey! Say! JUMP member Arioka Daiki (also affiliated with Johnny & Associates).[10] The 2020 film *Stigmatized Properties* (*Jiko bukken*, dir. Nakata Hideo) featured Kamenashi Kazuya, a member of the popular band Kat-Tun, who was the subject of a lengthy interview and photo spread in the film magazine *Kinema Junpō*, while promotion for the 2021 film *Suicide Forest Village* (discussed in chapter 3) featured an upbeat pop song by girl group FAKY. Such connections between Japanese horror films and the world of popular singers, models, actors, and *tarento* are not entirely new—popular actors Matsushima Nanako and Sanada Hiroyuki starred in the original *Ringu* film; actress and model Koyuki starred in *Pulse*; and *Dark Water*, *One Missed Call*, and *Pulse* all featured the somewhat jarring addition of upbeat pop songs playing over their end credits. Still, in the 2010s and beyond, the marketing of Japanese horror films has become much more focused on the presence of these songs and pop stars, with magazine features, tweets, and video clips heavily focused on photos of the stars and their public image.

Japanese horror films of the 2010s and beyond are also still very much in touch with the themes and visual motifs that defined them during the "boom" period of the late 1990s and early 2000s: demonic children (*Innocent Curse*, *Howling Village* [*Inunaki mura*, dir. Takashi Shimizu 2020]), the breakdown of family and social support networks (*Creepy*), and a reliance on an atmosphere of eeriness and dread rather than gore or jump-scares (*The Inerasable* [*Zan-e: Sunde wa ikenai heya*, dir. Nakamura Yoshihiro 2015]; *Our House* [*Watashitach no ie*, dir. Kiyohara Yui 2018]; and *Bilocation* [*Bairokēshon*, dir. Asato Mari 2013]). But where films like *Ringu* and *Pulse* focused on "media anxiety" surrounding tension between original and copy, or the question of whether the digital world was "real," contemporary Japanese horror films exist in a dramatically different media universe, one in which many of us are savvy enough to realize that "authenticity" is a heavily fictionalized concept, and where the word "real" has many different meanings. Not surprisingly, the idea that reality is a nebulous concept, or that supernatural monsters might just be a hallucination brought on by stress, has become more prominent in Japanese horror films in recent years (perhaps taking a cue from many successful United States, European, and Australian horror films that have explored similar themes).[11] This tension is explored not only in Japan via the "mockumentary" and found-footage format (particularly the films of Shiraishi Kōji, including *Shirome* [2010], discussed in chapter 2) but also through films that present stories of heavily fictionalized "real" places or events (*Howling Village*, *Toshimaen: The Movie* [discussed in chapter 1], *Suicide Forest Village* [discussed in chapter 3]), creating an experience in which both audience and characters exist in a "fractured reality." Shaped and circulated via new media technologies, these films use the appearance of realness to create something that feels authentic. Those who engage with such films have become skilled at embracing this aura of authenticity to enhance their own experience, even if they are also savvy enough to know that it is fiction.

OLD/NEW MEDIA, VIRTUAL WINDOWS, AND JAPANESE HORROR

In their introduction to *Media Theory in Japan* (2017), Steinberg and Zahlten trace media theory from its early days to "the rise of 'new media' in the 1990s" to the more recent "media studies" of Lisa Gitelman, Jonathan Sterne, Alexander Galloway, and Jussi Parikka that has "shifted to analyses of formats, platforms, media objects, and materialities" (31). Steinberg and Zahlten argue that "moments of new media are often moments of new developments in media theory" (30). The invention of new media devices and objects, in other words, naturally leads to new ways of speaking about, analyzing, or knowing them. Within the context of media theory and media studies, though, how exactly do we define "new" media? Lev Manovich argues that "that which is distributed by a computer" is too limiting, instead proposing that new media represents "the translation of all existing media into numerical data accessible through computers" (Manovich 2001, 19–20). The result is "graphics, moving images, sounds, shapes, spaces, and texts that have become computable; that is, they comprise simply another set of computer data" (20). Wendy Hui Kyong Chun, though, cautions against granting too much "stability" to a term like "new media," arguing that "computation does not automatically lead to new media or software" (Chun 2016a, 3). From the spread of its usage in the 1990s, the term "portrayed other media as old or dead" (Chun 2016a, 2). It "was not mass media, specifically television. It was fluid, individualized connectivity, a medium to distribute control and freedom."[12] It was not simply "digital media" or "digitized forms of other media . . . but rather an interactive medium or form of distribution as independent as the information it relayed" (Chun 2016a, 2).

The "new" of new media is the subject of much debate—Henry Jenkins argues that "old media never die—and they don't even necessarily fade away. What dies are simply the tools we use to access the media content" (Jenkins 2006, 13). Old media are not necessarily being displaced by new media, but rather, "their functions and status are shifted by the introduction of new technologies" (14). All media were new at some point, newness "contains within itself repetition," and making something new posits "the transformation of something known and familiar into something wonderful," which means that "'making new' reveals the importance of interrogating the forces behind any emergence" (Chun 2016a, 4). Old media is static, new media is constantly changing; old media is passive, new media is interactive. New media are "wonderfully creepy" because they "mess with the distinction between publicity and privacy, gossip, and political speech, surveillance and entertainment, intimacy and work, hype and reality" (Chun 2016b, ix).

In summary, in as much as the concept can be concisely defined, "new media" refers to a particular group of media objects (videos, images, games, and virtual reality environments) that are primarily produced and distributed through devices such as computers and smart phones and that are further defined by variability, "fluid, individualized connectivity," and a certain amount of interactivity, particularly when compared to more "passive" media such as television, books, and photographs. And yet conclusively defining new media and what makes it "new" or different from old media remains a very slippery prospect, particularly given that media exist in a "cycle of obsolescence" and that most forms of "new" media "will inevitably disappoint and be replaced by something else that promises, once again, the new" (Chun 2016a, 1). The newness of new media is ephemeral, ghostly in much the same way that so many forms of electronic media have been described as ghostly or "haunted" with "electronic presence" (Sconce 2000) since their inception.

In discussing the role of old and new media in Japanese horror films, it is also important to examine the literal and figurative frames that surround their narratives (and that appear as smaller frames-within-frames in the films themselves). Andre Bazin's essay "Cinema and Painting" begins as an examination of films that depict paintings, but it is also an exploration of the concept of the frame and what it depicts. For Bazin, a framed painting

> is separated off not only from reality as such but, even more so, from the reality that is represented in it. Indeed it is a mistake to see a picture frame as having merely a decorative or rhetorical function . . . The essential role of the frame is, if not to create at least to emphasize the difference between the microcosm of the picture and the macrocosm of the natural world in which the painting has come to take its place. (Bazin 2005 [1967], 165)

The frame "offers a space the orientation of which is inwards, a contemplative area opening solely onto the interior of the painting" (166). A frame is a window onto another world, and the painting within it represents not reality as such, but a mediated version of it. What is included within the frame is a component of that mediated reality, and what is outside of it is not. Sayad (2016) argues that even within a movie theater, "the film is never fully contained within the silver screen" thanks to advances in sound and 3D technology (47). In horror films, and found footage horror films in particular, the filmic frame "invites considerations about both the harboring of monsters off-screen and the dangers lurking in the dark corners of a delimited visual field" (48). Whether viewed in a theater or on a variety of digital media devices, contemporary Japanese horror films generate fear by pushing the boundaries of frame and screen, sometimes through the use of 3D technology, and sometimes through a layering of screens and frames that confuses notions of inside/outside and film world/online world.

In *The Virtual Window*, Anne Friedberg builds on Bazin and others to move between analyses of perspective in painting, the architectural window, the technology of glass-making, the concept of vision and perspective, and the development of the "windows" computer interface to imagine the *virtual* window, a layered concept that combines the frame, the film screen, the computer "window," and the architectural window:

> As images move across the screens of cinema, television, and the computer, the viewer's immobility meets a paradoxical and compensatory mobility when moving images are seen within a frame. As screens contain other screens in a nested *mise en abyme* of multiple frames, as quattrocento

perspective is both fractured and multiplied, the "virtual window" opens onto a new logic of visuality, a time-architecture, framed and virtual, on a screen. (Friedberg 2006, 18)

Friedberg's "nested *mise en abyme*" of frames, screens, and windows is vividly illustrated in the narratives and images central to the films under discussion in this book, as well as in the manner of their dissemination and consumption.

Japanese horror films of the 2010s and beyond also present us with an endless series of interfaces. We watch these films on a variety of new media devices, and on our large and small screens we often see others viewing film footage through large and small screens, their reflections mixing with our own. Such interfaces are "ultimately something beyond the screen. . . . [The] social field itself constitutes a grand interface, an interface between subject and world, between surface and source, and between critique and the objects of criticism" (Galloway 2012, 54). In the "nested" frames and screens that are visible to us both in the images and the production/dissemination processes of so many later Japanese horror films, we can also see layers of mediation, porous barriers between the spectator and the thing being viewed.

Frames, screens, windows, and interfaces exacerbate a sense of uncertainty as to what is real or authentic in the media that we consume. Long before social media and smart phones made engagement with media a constant feature of everyday life for many, Baudrillard had argued that the world was defined by a "completely new species of uncertainty, which results not from the lack of information but from information itself and even from an excess of information," and that the uncertainty this excess of information produced was "irreparable" (Baudrillard 2016 [1985], 517). Similarly, in the early 2000s Anne Friedberg argued that "a variety of screens . . . compete for our attention without any convincing arguments about hegemony . . . the window's metaphoric boundary is no longer the singular frame of perspective" (Friedberg 2006, 242–243). In today's media landscape, we constantly look and are looked at, with images, text, and videos easily remediated and shared between a variety of platforms and devices. The everyday lives of both the famous and the ordinary are regularly served up as an all-consuming spectacle, a quintessential feature of modern life, "the sun which never sets over the empire of modern passivity." Spectacle "covers the entire surface of the world and bathes endlessly in its own glory" (Debord 1995 [1967], 13). The perspectives of Debord, Michel de Certeau (on the way that human activity shapes urban space), and Jean Baudrillard (on the nature of reality and simulation) are invaluable in an age when media spectacle has reached levels of saturation that all of these thinkers predicted and yet could not have foreseen: a time in which humans and media-manufactured realities are engaged in an endless feedback loop via devices (smart phones, tablets) that allow us (or force us) to be eternally plugged in.

For the purposes of this book, I am particularly interested in Japanese horror films' depiction of this "spectacle" and of new media technologies/devices, specifically the depiction of video-sharing sites like YouTube and Niconico, online forums like 2channel, social media platforms like Twitter and Instagram, and new media devices such as computers, tablets, and smart phones. As they are depicted in numerous Japanese horror films from the 2010s and beyond, these devices and technologies contribute to the sense of "fractured reality" inherent in the films' narratives, both through their roles in the films themselves and in the way that they have shaped audience perceptions of certain images and ideas. In the film *Toshimaen: The Movie* (discussed in chapter 1), which features a cracked smart phone screen as its movie poster, malevolent forces are set in motion through a Niconico video and a personal smart phone video. Characters question whether what they see in the videos is "real," while the film's narrative also mixes a real place (the Toshimaen amusement park) with an invented urban legend about the "Toshimaen curse."

In the film *Suicide Forest Village*, discussed in chapter 3, we see footage of a woman broadcasting live from the Aokigahara forest in a video that resembles many amateur videos that already exist on YouTube and Niconico. The scene is meant to be frightening, but the same actress also appears in a short, cheerful video touted as a "collaboration" with Yamanashi prefecture, ostensibly designed to introduce Aokigahara to the public in a less frightening way. One description of the video on YouTube encourages viewers to check out the "real" Fuji sea of trees (*hontō no Fuji no jukai*) after watching the movie (Movie Collection 2021). In both of these films, including online video "windows" within the film frame forces the viewer and the characters to constantly question the authenticity of what they are experiencing. The ubiquity of screens and virtual windows in our daily lives means that "the limits and multiplicities of our frames of vision determine the boundaries and multiplicities of our world . . . [We] now receive images . . . in spatially and temporally fractured frames" (Friedberg 2006, 7). In the years since Anne Friedberg analyzed these "virtual windows," screens—giant, small, moving, still—are so common in a city like Tokyo as to be ignored by most passersby, truly "matter(ing) most when they seem not to matter at all" (Chun 2016b, 1). Via these many layers of frames, windows, and screens, Japanese horror films force us to constantly shift our perception, to constantly question the framing of what we see.

The role of new media technologies and devices in Japanese horror—in circulating images and ideas, in serving as characters in their own right in films, in their use as marketing and promotional tools—also points to their inherent spectrality. Long before the concept of "new media" existed, the ability of certain forms of "old" media to manipulate our sense of time, to "capture" images and preserve them, and to present images that seemed simultaneously tangible and fleeting made them inherently ghostly. Media "always already provide the appearance of specters" (Kittler 1999 [1986], 12). The worlds created by electronic media "often evoke the supernatural by creating virtual beings that appear to have no physical form," with telephones, radios, and computers often seen as "'possessed' [by] 'ghosts in the machine,' the technologies serving as either uncanny electronic agents or as gateways to electronic otherworlds" (Sconce 2000, 4). In the world of new media in particular, one "based in the proliferation of virtual images, the concept of the phantasm gains new valency as an element of the cultural imaginary" (Gunning 2013, 211). Cinema and photography themselves, from their earliest incarnations in the form of daguerrotypes and magic lantern shows, presented us with images that "oscillate(d) between visibility and invisibility, presence and absence, materiality and immateriality" (Gunning 2013, 212).

Japanese horror films have also often been fascinated by the inherent spectrality of practices like spirit photography (*shinrei shashin*). Before *Ringu*, the 1988 film *Psychic Vision* (*Jaganrei*, dir. Ishii Teruyoshi, discussed in chapter 2) depicted a pop star haunted by ghostly images of another woman that showed up in photos. In a film often seen as a blueprint for *Ringu*, *Don't Look Up* (*Joyūrei*, dir. Nakata Hideo 1996, discussed in chapter 4), the actual celluloid used during a film shoot appears to be "haunted" by the presence of a dead actress and a film from the past. In *Ringu*, photographic images of Sadako's victims appear distorted on the photo paper, and, as mentioned previously, characters seem to transform into film negatives in their final, terrified moments. And in *Pulse*, grainy images of hooded figures appear in the dim screens of computers, appearing as seemingly insubstantial spirits in the "real" world but then revealing themselves to be tangible. On the subject of "digital horror," Blake and Aldana Reyes argue that "If a fear of technology and the machine has lurked in horror for a long time—even inflecting its presentation—then digital horror makes this terror explicit and turns it into both an aesthetic and a narrative preoccupation" (Blake and Aldana Reyes 2015, 16). Ghostly characters and objects in films like *Pulse* are doubly spectral: they are ghosts or spirits not only within the narrative but also by virtue of the fact that they exist within a form of technology that has always been connected to spectrality.

This spectrality becomes even more pronounced when the screens in question are connected to new media devices and technologies—to video-streaming services, social media platforms, virtual reality environments, and smartphone screens. On a basic level, there is the ephemerality of the new media object—unlike a paper photograph or a video cassette tape, videos and photographs circulated online are less tangible, easily appearing and disappearing from one platform to another. But in the same moment that they are ephemeral, they are also less easily disposed of—digital images and videos are easily copied and shared, appearing again and again in different forms and on different platforms. Deleting means little—as one character points out in *Sadako 3D* (discussed in chapter 4), videos that are unavailable on the Niconico video-sharing site remain on the site's server, allowing them the potential to be copied and uploaded elsewhere at any time. The lack of a clear origin and the ease of copying/editing these videos and images contributes to a sense of uncertainty regarding how "real" they are—like ghosts, these new media objects seem to be able to appear and disappear at will, presenting themselves as simultaneously material and immaterial. In *Sadako 3D*, students search for a cursed video on their smart phones but repeatedly see "404 file not found" messages or instead click on "prank" videos. Their sense of perspective (and ours) is also constantly shifting: the film begins with a live Niconico broadcast that appears framed within a smart phone screen, which is then shown on other characters' computer screens, which are then framed within whatever screen the viewer is using to watch the film. Even if, as spectators, we are now savvy enough to know that what we are watching is not "real," the constant shifting between screens, frames, and new media formats means that our sense of reality also shifts, and we are forced to literally and figuratively reframe our expectations.

In the year 2000, Jeffrey Sconce argued that media had long been described as "haunted" by electronic presence, depicted as "an electronic maelstrom where a ceaselessly mediated and ultimately phantom public sphere exists interwoven with the eternally unfolding diegesis of a thousand worlds in television's ever-expanding universe of syndication" (Sconce 2000, 11). At that time, Sconce was primarily writing about TV and radio—the Internet had not yet become the all-consuming force that it is today. Surely now these "shared, electronically generated worlds of national programming" are even more woven into the fabric of our daily lives via international streaming, video sharing, and social media. And we now live in a world where much of our media has lost its tangibility—rather than DVD, VHS cassette, and hard disk, our content comes to us via virtual "clouds" of data, more often than not accessed via a phone or computer rather than a movie theater or TV screen. Our physical relationship to the technology—slipperier and slipperier—mirrors the nature of our relationship to reality and authenticity through media, which gets harder and harder to pin down.

Haunting and spectrality, then, are features not only of the narratives of contemporary Japanese horror films but also are in fact woven into the technologies that produce and disseminate these films, and into the mediaverse in which they exist. These digital ghosts and ghostly spaces are infused with both absence and presence—they present new media objects that feel ephemeral in comparison to their old media object counterparts, but in their potential for endless circulation and reproducibility, they also refuse to be forgotten. In their spectrality, they force us to "doubt this reassuring order or presents and, especially, the border between the present, the actual or present reality of the present, and everything that can be opposed to it" (Derrida 1994, 40). As they exist in and around Japanese horror films, new media objects and technologies not only manipulate our sense of past, present, and future but also force us to question our sense of order and perspective, "haunting" the technological means through which the films are shaped and circulated and the narrative worlds that they depict.

METHODOLOGY AND PRIMARY TEXTS

As the title of this volume indicates, my concern in this book is with Japanese horror films, how they are circulated (and reshaped/reinterpreted), and how the presence of new media objects within and around their narratives contributes to a sense of fractured reality. My primary texts are feature films, but my analysis also draws on YouTube videos, internet urban legends, manga, and film paratexts (publicity stunts, ad copy, film reviews) that in some way touch on the themes of haunting, ghosts, or monsters. In examining this particular group of texts through the lenses of J-horror cinema studies, new media studies, and cultural studies, I hope to reveal the ways that Japanese horror films continue to frighten, entertain, and wrestle with complicated issues, in a media landscape where their overall effect is further complicated (and in some ways enhanced) by changes in technology. Such technology both serves as a source of anxiety in horror media narratives and, in the "real" world, is central to how those narratives are shaped and disseminated.

Chapter 1 looks at the depiction of "net lore" in Japanese horror films, examining these stories' journeys from message boards like the 2channel "Occult" forum to DVD series and feature films. I focus on the "digital urban legend" of *Kunekune* (a story that first appeared online in the early 2000s), the depiction of 2channel via a multitude of screens in the *2channel Curse* (*2channeru no noroi*, 2010-2013, various directors) DVD and film series, and the "invented" urban legend depicted in the film *Toshimaen: The Movie*. I look at how the Internet and social media have changed the way that Japanese urban legends spread and evolve, as well as how new media objects, computer/smartphone screens, and a tension between older and newer forms of media have become central to many Japanese horror films from the 2010s and beyond. These films depict not only the (invented) urban legends themselves but also characters' engagement with 2channel and Niconico videos, shifting perspectives between computer screens, smartphone screens, and the larger film frame. Watching these films on a smartphone or computer effectively makes the viewer part of the chain of mediation—we watch others interacting with a computer or smartphone in much the same way that we do as we watch the film. Looking at the extent to which many of these films foreground the presence of old and new media devices, we can see the inherent spectrality not only of the ghosts and spirits that populate these stories but also the media devices and technologies through which they are disseminated and consumed.

Chapter 2 examines Japanese horror's connections to the found-footage horror genre with a focus on the film *Shirome* (with a brief discussion of the 1988 film *Psychic Vision*), examining how the appearance of realness blends with fiction to create an "authentic" experience in the context of two distinct media spaces: found footage horror films and Japanese pop idol culture. I argue that these two worlds are linked by the concept of the "mutual agreement" (*o-yakusoku*)—an agreement between fans and creators that certain illusions of intimacy and reality will not be questioned. Seen through a mix of POVs, frames, and media devices, the collections of "found" footage that make up the narratives in these films draw our attention not only to what is visible, but to what is invisible or blurred. Ultimately, *Shirome* reveals the "spatially and temporally fractured frames" (Friedberg 2006, 7) through which spectators connect to the worlds of both Japanese found footage horror and the Japanese idol. The frequent juxtaposition of handheld camera footage, portable DVD players, and oral storytelling in the film further illustrates the changes in how ghost stories are shared.

Chapter 3 looks not only within Japan but also outside of it, with a focus on depictions of Aokigahara, the forest at the base of Mount Fuji that has long been associated with suicide. I examine depictions of Aokigahara in both Japanese and English-language journalism, YouTube videos, and films, focusing specifically on the 2021 Japanese film *Suicide Forest Village* and the 2015 English-language horror film *The Forest* (dir. Jason Zada). Both films make use of a multitude of screens and "virtual windows" that force the viewer to frequently shift perspective and question the authenticity of what they are seeing. In the case of *The Forest*, Aokigahara's status as a real place imbues it with a particular type of "authentic aura" for horror film consumers and creators, but the "reality" of Aokigahara that is presented on screen is heavily Orientalized, imagining the forest as a literal black hole of otherness that swallows its non-Japanese protagonists. In the case of *Suicide Forest Village*, layers of reality and fantasy are further complicated by the role of new media objects within the film's narrative and the presence of MX4D technology in movie theaters, as well as an "official" collaboration with

Yamanashi prefecture that features one of the actresses from the film. Both films reveal the ways that fragments of Aokigahara are circulated, reshaped, and endlessly mediated both inside and outside Japan, creating a final film product that presents a fractured sense of reality.

Chapter 4 traces the genesis and evolution of the *Ringu* franchise, beginning with an analysis of the ways that Nakata Hideo's *Don't Look Up* and *Ringu* imagine ghostly invasions of the empty spaces within the physical objects of celluloid and videocassette tapes. I then focus on three later *Ringu* sequels and remakes: *Sadako 3D*, *Sadako*, and *Rings*. In these films, produced during a time when smartphone, social media, and computer usage was much more widespread than during the time of the initial *Ringu* films' releases, we see the ways that literal and figurative frames become even more interactive, inviting the films' characters and spectators to fall into screens, or sending projectiles hurtling toward them out of the screen. Via the wide circulation of the image of Sadako in films, humorous manga, promotional videos, and live publicity stunts, I illustrate the ways in which Sadako, like her cursed video, has become an easily reproducible and remediated commodity, "infecting" different platforms and devices as she moves easily from screen to screen and universe to universe. As with *Shirome*, in these films the juxtaposition of newer and older media devices and technologies also reveals changes in how ghost stories are told, shared, and reshaped.

My conclusion attempts to put these varied analyses in a particular historical and cultural context, with an eye to the new role that "virtual windows" have come to play in our everyday lives since the COVID-19 pandemic began in early 2020. During this period filmmakers and media content creators, including horror filmmakers, were forced to find creative new ways to produce their content, from "remote" film shoots edited together and shared online to horror films that take place entirely within a Zoom meeting. Given that so many of us have often been confined within the screens that are our only means of connecting with other humans, I argue that Japanese horror, particularly horror that centers on new media, takes on a new level of meaning in a world where many of us find ourselves engaging not only with film and video but with the entirety of the outside world as a whole, via an endless series of screens and frames.

Sadako began her filmic existence within the frame of a TV screen, shared both within the *Ringu* narrative and in the larger world via the now-obsolete medium of videocassettes. Her various incarnations in the 2020s—LINE sticker, bubble tea advertisement, cuddly comic book character—mirror the shifts in Japanese horror films' depiction of new media technologies and their many types of screens. The telling of scary stories, once primarily an oral tradition, has now become a practice of sharing digital images and words across multiple platforms, a practice that has found its way into the narratives of horror films themselves. Fear is circulated in an endless loop, the frames and screens that once limited the ghosts now more porous, allowing for movement across media forms, devices, and narrative worlds.

NOTES

1. After introducing both the original Japanese titles of films and their English-language translations, I will refer to Japanese films by their English-language titles. However, in the case of *Ringu*, I will refer to the 1998 Japanese film as *Ringu* and its 2002 U.S. remake as *The Ring*.

2. Unless otherwise indicated, all translations are my own.

3. Japanese names are written family name first, given name second.

4. Lev Manovich uses the term "new media object" to refer to objects that "may be a digital still, digitally composited film, virtual 3-D environment, computer game, self-contained hypermedia DVD," essentially "graphics, moving images, sounds, shapes, spaces, and texts that have become computable" (Manovich 2001, 14, 20).

5. As defined by Jonathan Gray (building on the work of Gerard Genette), paratexts include promotional materials, toys, games, publicity stunts, and fan-produced content connected to a primary text such as a film or novel. These paratexts are both separate from and "intrinsically part of" any text—they "are not simply add-ons, spinoffs, and also-rans: they create texts, they manage them, and they fill them with many of the meanings that we associate with them" (Gray 2010, 6).

6. Maekawa (2015), Brown (2015), Kinoshita (2009), McRoy (2005), and others use the term "J-horror" primarily to refer to a group of films made in the late 1990s and early 2000s, including the *Ringu* and *Grudge* series and several films by director Kurosawa Kiyoshi, several of which were remade in the United States. Throughout this book, I will use the term "J-horror" when referencing the words of these and other scholars, and when referring to the "brand" of Japanese horror that developed in the late 1990s and early 2000s. In other contexts, though, I will use the phrase "Japanese horror films" to reflect the slightly wider scope of the stories and styles of the films under examination in this book.

7. Though they share the same phonetic name, the screenwriter and film scholar Takahashi Hiroshi and the director of *Toshimaen: The Movie* (also named Takahashi Hiroshi) are in fact two different people (their given names are written with different kanji).

8. Dumas' analysis here is primarily focused on the *Ringu* novel, but I think that this theme of repetition is also very much present in the film.

9. The idea that many Japanese films are low-risk ventures produced for established fan bases comes through clearly in a conversation between directors, producers, and executives working in the Japanese film industry held in 2021. The director Yukisada Isao comments on what it was like to have one of his films released via streaming on Amazon instead of only in theaters (due to pandemic-related safety issues). He mentions that this film received more online reviews than any of his previous films, and expresses surprise that many of the reviews were "very harsh,"

adding that this might be the first time that large numbers of people who were not a part of his usual fanbase sought out one of his films (Tokyo International Film Festival 2021).

10. Shortly before and after the film's release, Takizawa and Arioka were the subjects of covers and glossy photo spreads in *Cinema Square*, *Nihon Eiga Navi*, *Shūkan TV Guide*, *Shūkan Monthly TV Fan*, and *An An*.

11. Examples of English-language films from the 2010s and beyond that focus on uncertainty about whether the threat is real or imagined, or simply create a hallucinatory atmosphere in which hallucination and "reality" are hard to distinguish, include *The Babadook* (dir. Jennifer Kent 2014), *Get Out* (dir. Jordan Peele 2017), *Annihilation* (dir. Alex Garland 2018), *Relic* (dir. Natalie Erika James 2020), and *The Invisible Man* (dir. Leigh Whannell 2020). For his part, director Nakata Hideo noted in a 2020 interview with *Kinema Junpō* that he has noticed the increasing popularity in Japan of Halloween celebrations and the success of films like *It*, and that he pays close attention to the kinds of non-Japanese horror films that are growing in popularity both inside and outside Japan (Matsuzaki 2020, 16).

12. Chun notes that "new media" is a "plural noun often treated as a singular subject," with new media scholars designating it as an "it" or a "they" depending on the context (Chun 2016a, 2). In general in this book, I will refer to "new media" the concept/term as singular and the technologies as plural. I will also occasionally borrow Manovich's "new media objects" to refer to specific images, videos, or pieces of texts circulated via the Internet and social media.

Chapter 1

Circulating Urban Legends
From 2channel to Toshimaen: The Movie

Zenshōan Temple, located in Sendagi, on the eastern side of Tokyo, is the final resting place of the famous *rakugo* performer Sanyutei Enchō, known in particular for his performances of ghost stories, a long summer tradition in Japan. Enchō was also known for his large collection of *yūrei-zu*, or "ghost paintings," paintings that both depict images of ghosts and ghostly phenomena and are said to be haunted by the spirit of a deceased person. Given their associations with death and dark subject matter, *yūrei-zu* are not frequently on display to the public and tend to be kept out of sight, often at temples, considered to be one of the safest places to store them.

Every August, though, Zenshōan Temple displays an assortment of Enchō's paintings to the public. At one time, this exhibition coincided with another summer tradition, the *hyakumonogatari kaidankai*, or a gathering for the telling of a hundred ghost stories. That tradition, which began in the Edo period, takes place at night and involves lighting one hundred wicks in an *andon* lamp and extinguishing one each time a story is told. As the night continues, "the room becomes darker and darker . . . and the atmosphere becomes ghostly" (Asai 1910, 145, quoted in Reider 2000, 267). August, it seems, is the time of year when certain kinds of frightening images and concepts are given free rein and brought out into the light, when otherwise taboo topics become appropriate for discussion, and in some cases even take on a playful, silly quality. On a typical exhibition day, the tiny display room in Zenshōan Temple will likely be crowded with mostly older visitors. On the walls are images of vengeful female spirits, ghostly musicians, mournful-looking women, and skulls. Some are truly frightening, like the image of a skeletal, bloody warrior holding a baby, or a woman holding a man's severed head. Outside the room, the temple gift shop sells books of art prints, postcards, and T-shirts and pens printed with simple line drawings of a skull.

Zenshōan is located in the neighborhood of Yanaka, which by the late 2010s had become a small-scale tourist attraction thanks to its well-preserved shops that project an aura of decades past. Fresh sembei are on sale, there are shops selling geta, and local cafes serve shaved ice and mochi with red bean desserts in rooms that look spirited out of the Taishō era. Looking at ghost paintings in a neighborhood that evokes nostalgia, one might recall that ghosts and monsters in Japan have frequently been associated with an urban-rural divide, and with a nostalgic, mythic pastoral—for many people the "real" Japan—always existing in tension with a modern, urban Japan. For scholars like Gerald Figal and Michael Dylan Foster, folk monsters like *yōkai*, a category that includes various entities that range from mischievous to genuinely dangerous, are for many people connected with this idealized rural landscape, while other kinds of monsters, like *kuchi-sake-onna* (the "slit-mouthed woman") represent the dangers and alienation of the city (Figal 2000; Foster 2008).

Seeing physical paintings of ghosts in an actual gallery and attending an in-person storytelling event is also a reminder of the extent to which the spreading of scary stories in Japan has moved from the analog to the digital. *Hyakumonogatari kaidankai* events began as in-person events and still take that form, but they have also been made into films and TV specials. In the 2010s and beyond, we often view these ghosts through computer or smartphone screens that link us to "copy-pasted" stories on popular scary story forums or images of creatures like "Momo," a sculpture inspired by a monster from Japanese folklore that spread, along with rumors of its dangers, via social media. Old media never truly die, and older media forms are not "killed" by new ones—rather, old media "functions and status are shifted by the introduction of new technologies" (Jenkins 2006, 14). The telling of ghost stories, whether in the form of in-person events, television programs, or texts exchanged in Internet forums, continues unabated, mixing older media forms with faster and more efficient means of delivery.

A variety of literal and figurative frames surround Japanese ghost stories, both in terms of the screens through which those stories are disseminated and the media devices that are depicted within Japanese horror films. We might access an urban legend through a feature film (seen in a theater, on a TV set via a DVD player, or on our computer screen via streaming), via an online "scary stories" message board (accessed via our smartphones or computers), or via a YouTube or Niconico video (accessed similarly, with an opportunity for more active, real-time participation in the case of Niconico). More interactive platforms like Niconico and YouTube "turn a viewer into an active user" in the way that *"new media turn most images into image-interfaces and image-instruments.* The image becomes interactive, that is, it now functions as an interface between a user and a computer or other devices" (Manovich

2001, 183, emphasis in original). Users may view frightening images or stories on a wide variety of screens and then easily share those images or stories (or their own comments on them), both reshaping and circulating ghost stories across different platforms and communication devices. And the frame/screen through which one experiences these stories has a powerful influence on the experience: "it is not narrative and not the optics of projection that recenter the spectator, but the frame itself. It is the consistency of the frame that performs the unity of space, not narrative. Even in films where shots are geometrically variant, the frame positions the viewer." (Friedberg 2006, 84). Our position as a viewer, and our perceived separation from the narrative via the supposed boundary of the screen and the frame, is made more uncertain in the presence of new media devices and objects.

In the case of Japan, many modern scary stories and urban legends originated on what was at one time arguably the country's largest and most influential online message board, 2channel, a chaotic collection of discussion threads on almost every topic imaginable. Much "net lore" was born on and shaped by 2channel and its successors' particular architecture and customs. Even the ghost stories that did not originate on the site may eventually be found there, shaped and reshaped by the 2channel framework. Where urban legends and ghost stories were once spread primarily by word of mouth or old media such as newspaper and television, since the early 2000s they have been shared and shaped primarily on the Internet, and specifically on websites that foster very particular types of stories and community experiences. Their appearance in films, in turn, has often incorporated the presence of certain digital technologies and websites, while the films' marketing has often emphasized a connection to the "realness" of these stories. The images of personal computers, smartphones, and video images framed within those devices, often presented as ghostly lights in the darkness, points to the inherent spectrality of digital media.

This chapter examines the circulation and framing of the Japanese urban legend through its dissemination and consumption via different types of media platforms and media devices, as well as its depiction in Japanese horror films, which often foreground images of media devices like computer screens and smartphones. I examine the concept of "net lore" and the urban legend of *Kunekune*, as well as the depiction of 2channel urban legends in the DVD and film collection *2channel Curse* (*2channeru no noroi* 2010–2013, various directors). Finally, I look at the "invented" urban legend of *Toshimaen: The Movie* (*Eiga: Toshimaen* 2019, dir. Takahashi Hiroshi), a film which exists at the nexus of multiple forms of new and old media and, like so many urban legends, juxtaposes nostalgia for a mythic version of the past with uneasiness about new media technologies and devices. Looking at the way that frightening images and narratives have been circulated, as well as the extent to which many films about them foreground images of old and new media devices, we can see the inherent spectrality not only of the ghosts and spirits that populate these stories but also the media devices and technologies through which they are disseminated and consumed. The presence of so many media devices, as well as the frequent juxtaposition of old and new media, illustrates the changes in how scary stories are told and shared. When such telling and circulation via new media devices happens both within the films *and* via their marketing campaigns and paratexts, diegetic borders created by screens and frames are further blurred.

YŌKAI, GHOST STORIES, AND THE OTHERWORLDLY

In the same way that urban legends have spread both through word of mouth and different types of media, older forms of Japanese folk tales have been passed from person to person and through plays, poetry, journalism, and novels. Central to much of this folklore is the category of the *yōkai*, a group of supernatural beings that include creatures such as the *kappa* (a green, humanoid creature with webbed hands and feet that supposedly lives in rivers) and more human-like beings such as *kuchi-sake-onna*, the slit-mouthed woman (a woman who wears a mask and terrorizes children by removing it to reveal a slit mouth). Historically, *yōkai* have been used to explain all manner of unusual phenomena, "a mechanism for contending with the unknown and its potential dangers" (Foster 2009, 11). *Yōkai* have also always existed as both generally frightening and simply troublesome, or even cute: "A *yōkai* may signify something wild and frightening, but removed from its natural environment, it becomes sanitized and safe enough to be handled by children . . . [The] same *yōkai* can exist simultaneously . . . as an object of fear and an object of amusement" (Foster 2009, 12). Komatsu Kazuhiko argues that *yōkai* culture "is not a relic of the past; it remains an inseparable part of modern culture . . . In fact, it's not an exaggeration to say that a deeper knowledge of *yōkai* is a prerequisite for a deeper understanding of Japanese culture as a whole" (Komatsu 2017, 6).

Figal, Foster, and Komatsu have noted that Japanese ghosts and monsters, and *yōkai* in particular, have long been associated with an urban-rural divide in Japan. *Yōkai* are frequently connected to rural Japan and a nostalgic vision not only of an agrarian past but also to "backward" ways of thinking and superstitions—Komatsu notes that when he first began his research on *yōkai* "many still considered *yōkai* superstitions that hindered the progress of Japanese civilization, and few saw any merit in investigating these forgotten relics of the past" (Komatsu 2017, 5). This was particularly true during the Meiji period, when reformers sought to "de-fang" folk monsters and superstitions by promoting rationalism and science in order to remake Japan in the shape of a truly "modern" nation. One example of this was the banning of certain kinds of *misemono* in the entertainment districts: street-based, low-brow entertainments like freak shows and haunted houses were banned and replaced with more "modern" amusements like the cinematograph and the vaudeville house, which also took these "popular performers and the crowds they attracted . . . off the open streets (historically the space of revolutionary action) and contained within a controlled economy of structures" (Figal 2000, 26). Figal also notes that *rakugo* performers, including Sanyutei Enchō, were likely pressured to change some of their ghost stories and hint that the visions of ghosts were caused by nervous disorders (*shinkei-byō*) (27-28). Art forms such as *rakugo* were thus used as instruments of the state to teach "enlightenment," reworking their stories so that they were about reason and science, not folk superstition.

Before this period, though, *rakugo* stories had frequently been centered around otherworldly and unlikely occurrences, whether in the form of extreme exaggeration or the appearance of supernatural phenomena. Morioka and Sasaki argue that *rakugo* relies on the juxtaposition of reality (*jitsu*) and unreality (*kyo*), where *kyo* "is not obvious at first glance, but takes shape gradually, and the principles of logic become weaker and weaker. At the other extreme of the spectrum, the world of *jitsu* openly turns upside down and becomes a chaotic mess" (Morioka and Sasaki 1990, 101). The "spectral world" is a key part of *kyo*: "This world and the eerie world of spectres are right next to one another. When depicted in a grotesque manner, the border between them vanishes, and all are free to come and go at will" (450). The function of this kind of grotesque entertainment as "a pointedly realistic denunciation of a sham reality. . . .is particularly evident during periods of social and political unrest," when the lower classes "tear off the veil of an already absurd reality by making it the object of their laughter. As a result, grotesque readily becomes a means of expression among the middle and lower classes in particular" (435-436).

Stories of fantastical creatures and worlds, then, sometimes served to draw attention to the absurdity of the *real* world, providing a means through which the lower and middle classes could express themselves. *Rakugo*'s particular brand of (often ghostly) storytelling, frequently featuring *yōkai*, has historically manipulated notions of real and unreal, transporting audiences to a world where the mundane and the supernatural exist side by side. It has also been used both as a tool of the state and as a form of protest against it, with those in power seeking to harness its influence to change people's thinking, and those with less power wielding it as a means to denounce the "sham reality" that those in power attempted to force on them. Like many forms of storytelling that feature monsters or ghosts, it has also wielded considerable influence in times of social rupture or crisis, with monsters standing in for the everyday uncertainties and anxieties that people were powerless to control. This manipulation of real and unreal, supernatural and mundane becomes even more pronounced when such stories are circulated via new media technologies, which are "wonderfully creepy" in the way that they "mess with the distinction between publicity and privacy, gossip and political speech, surveillance and entertainment, intimacy and work, hype and reality" (Chun 2016b, ix). Just as stories of the absurd blurred the line between real and unreal, absurd and rational, new media technologies as depicted in Japanese horror films enhance the ghostliness of horror narratives by blurring boundaries.

The *kaidan* (ghost story) has been told and passed down in many forms for hundreds of years in Japan—through oral tradition, theatrical performances, literature, radio, film, and television. Since the early 2000s, though, it has taken on a new life and shape via the Internet, and particularly through online discussion forums like 2channel and its successors, where some stories are born and then spread over the wider Internet, while some are brought in from other places and reshaped by the 2channel structure. As Nakayama notes, the creation and dissemination of "net lore" is varied and multidirectional—some stories are born on 2channel or other Internet forums and spread from there, and some may begin as oral narratives that are then posted and discussed on sites like 2channel (Nakayama 2016). And while these stories and their sharing may feel quite distant from the world of *rakugo*, many of the stories in question are strikingly similar to those popularized by *rakugo* performers, and they also rely on a similar juxtaposition of truth and fiction, to the point where fiction and reality become blurred.

Before examining representative examples of "net lore," it is helpful to first examine the genesis and structure of 2channel, where a large number of "Internet urban legends" originate. Founded in 1999 by the then twenty-three-year-old Nishimura Hiroyuki (who was studying abroad in Arkansas at the time and said he created the site because he was bored in his dorm room), the site had ten million daily users and received as many as 500 million page views a month in 2008 (Katayama 2008; Sakamoto 2011). Importantly, all 2channel users remain anonymous. According to Lisa Katayama, this makes the site an ideal place to vent about topics that no one feels comfortable speaking about openly in Japan. It's an "outlet for unfettered expression," a necessary release valve in a society where expressing contrary opinions openly is often frowned upon (Katayama 2008). Naturally, this means that the site is also full of hateful rhetoric—stories about 2channel tend to focus on the Internet's far right (*netto-uyoku*), Japanese nationalists who argue, among other things, that Koreans are inferior to Japanese and that the disputed Senkaku Islands should be returned to Japan.[1]

In its truly chaotic structure, with tens of thousands of discussion threads on a huge variety of topics, many of these discussions conducted using slang and ASCII art that make them incomprehensible to the outside user, 2channel generates a kind of digital cacophony that, for Itō Ryūhei, constitutes a "super urban space" (*chō toshi-teki kūkan*: Itō 2014, 4). If the city was one of the first places where large groups of people congregated and yet felt overwhelmed and isolated from each other, 2channel is that space in digital form. Itō calls it an "octopus community," a place where small groups of people congregate around a single "tentacle" but have no real idea what the other "tentacle" is doing—except during carnivalesque moments of "matsuri," when massive numbers of 2channel users swarm a particular bulletin board and momentarily cause the site to crash (Itō 2014, 8).

Kitada Akihiro argues that 2channel's primary mode of communication is snark and disdain: such communication is "intimate but harsh; the harshness is itself a kind of intimacy" (Kitada 2012, 70). 2channel users, who mostly grew up during the 1980s and experienced growing disillusionment with increasingly sensationalized "news," exhibit both a deep distrust of and scorn for mainstream media but also a deep love of it. Their very detailed "insider knowledge" created a "massive inner circle" defined by cynicism toward media. And yet, Kitada argues, as much as the average 2channeler may perform cynicism and scorn, they also have the ability to be moved by media, as evidenced by the *Train Man* phenomenon.[2] Performance seems to be key—whether they truly believe it or not, the *performance* of scorn and derision is key to the 2channel communication style, as is privileging the *act* of communication and the forming of social connections over actual *content*. Even young people in Japan who abhor or ignore 2channel still tend to communicate in a manner similar to 2channelers, with the mundane details of their everyday lives becoming fodder for endless communication between friends. As with 2channel discussions, the point is not necessarily the content (or the topic of those conversations), it's the communication and the social bonds themselves (Kitada 2012, 80).

If, as Marc Steinberg has argued, platform shapes content (Steinberg 2019), then the digital urban legends that arise out of the 2channel message boards are truly shaped by the environment of the site, particularly its architecture, which consists of mostly anonymous bulletin boards and threads that are limited to 1,000 posts each. Itō also notes that stories relayed on 2channel are "scrolling stories"—they are designed to be read as you scroll down lines of text on your computer or phone, meaning that the last line of the story is often the most important (Itō 2016, 24). The effect would be decidedly different if you printed the story and read it on paper. Another distinguishing feature of 2channel scary stories—and almost all Internet-based scary stories—is the copy-paste function, which means that there is often little variation in the stories themselves, with the exact text copied and pasted from website to website (in contrast to urban legends relayed via word of mouth, which have the potential to shift a great deal over time).[3] Interestingly, this perfect reproduction seems more likely to immediately reveal the story as "fake," since some variation in content would indicate that more than one person had heard (or experienced) the same story before sharing it. Still, as Nakayama notes, "net lore" may begin on the Internet, but it does not always stay there—stories born on the Internet can take on new life when they are picked up by other media outlets, and in those situations, we are more likely to see variations in content (Nakayama 2016).

Stories of monsters, ghosts, and the supernatural have long been circulated via word of mouth, television programs, newspaper articles, feature films, and online message boards. While the stories themselves may not change, their framing arguably changes the experience of sharing and hearing them. Mitsuyo Wada-Marciano notes that the materiality of visual media is important—J-horror as a genre in particular has long been connected more with DVDs than films screened in theaters (Wada-Marciano 2012, 47). In describing his experience of being utterly terrified by the found footage horror film *Psychic Vision*, to the point that he was extremely eager to return the video after finishing it, Takahashi Hiroshi makes a point of mentioning that he had watched the video alone, late at night, in his home (Takahashi 2004, 14). As we will see, the experience of sharing or learning about an urban legend via a computer or smartphone screen, which gives one access to a world both omnipresent and ephemeral, enhances the sense of "fractured reality" in these stories. Given that many of these stories circulate as new media objects, they are also imbued with a kind of digital spectrality, hovering constantly between absence and presence.

2CHANNEL AND "ELECTRIC" GHOST STORIES: *KUNEKUNE* AND *2CHANNEL CURSE*

On original 2channel message boards like "Occult" (*Okaruto*), users shared ghost stories and urban legends that in some cases had been passed around in digital and nondigital circles for a long time, and in others were born within 2channel itself. Itō Ryūhei describes these stories as "net lore," a term that first received public attention in Japan in 2000, when Ikeda Kayoko's book *If the World Were a Village of 100 People* (S*ekai ga moshi hyakunin no mura dattara*), based on a piece of "net lore" and an earlier article by environmentalist Donella Meadows, became a bestseller in Japan (Itō 2016; Ashby 2002). At that time, Ikeda described net lore as "a product of the internet's connecting system of gossip and legends, the channels that connect people and information, fact and fiction, gossip and legends" (Nakayama 2016, 124). Itō refers to net lore as *denshō*, a portmanteau that takes the traditional word for "folk tale" and replaces the first character for "den" (meaning "traditional") with the character for "electric," thus, *denshō*: "electric tales," or electric stories (Itō 2016, 78–79).

Electric tales are similar to urban legends, which folklorist Jan Harold Brunvand defines as having three primary characteristics: (1) they exist within the context of urban systems and culture, (2) they are always heard via a "friend of a friend" but never directly from the source, and (3) they are spread primarily not through word of mouth, but through media such as TV, radio, and newspapers (Nakayama 2016, 124). As early as 2001, Brunvand was also claiming that the primary method of dissemination for urban legends was the Internet (Brunvand 2001, xxvii). When it comes to Japanese *toshidensetsu* (literally "city legends"), many originate on 2channel threads, though the pathways of dissemination are not one-way: stories may be spread through old-fashioned word of mouth, but then take on new life when they are posted on 2channel (Nakayama 2016).[4] This is arguably what happened with the story of *kuchi-sake-onna*, the slit-mouthed woman, which began as a story spread among schoolchildren but then took on new life in newspapers, magazines, the Internet, and film (Foster 2009).

A common thread among many of these stories that begin on, or at least are primarily shared via 2channel message boards, is the illustration of an urban-rural divide. Many of the stories feature a protagonist who is a "city person" visiting the countryside (sometimes to visit family members), feeling out of sorts as a city person, and encountering something strange or frightening that they can't understand. In a story known as "Kinkisaki/Pandora," posted online in 2009 and on the 2channel "Occult" message board in 2011, children in a rural town are fascinated by an abandoned house that they call "Pandora," which their parents warn them against visiting or even talking about. When a young boy who has recently returned to the town from another prefecture (after his mother's divorce) encourages a group of them to check out the house, very bad things happen (Kaidan News-a). Various versions of the legend of Inunaki Tunnel imagine a remote tunnel that leads to an even more remote village that exists beyond the control of the Japanese government, or from which no one can return after they enter (CinemaCafe.net 2020). The messaging ties in with how supernatural phenomena and monsters have frequently been framed in Japan: as a part of the country's mythic, pastoral past, in contrast to the rational, urban present and future. These may be "urban" legends that are born via modern forms of technology, but they are still strongly tied to notions of the rural. Nakayama argues that this new concept of the countryside (*inaka*) as portrayed in digital urban legends has allowed a sort of digital *inaka*-space to flourish on the Internet, even as the actual inaka has faded and

Japan has become more known as a nation of large cities (Nakayama 2016, 123). Similarly, given that many social gathering spaces have moved into the digital realm, it makes sense that those spaces, like their real-world counterparts, would also eventually become "haunted," as Dickey argues:

> Social media sites like Facebook, Twitter, and Instagram have in many ways replaced (or at least complemented) the cafes, parks, and bars where we gather; it's little wonder, then, that they've also become populated with ghosts ... [As] with physical architecture, it's unlikely that we'll ever dispel these ghosts in the machine entirely; coding, after all, is a human endeavor, and like architecture, it's prone to a thousand variables that can never be fully controlled. (Dickey 2016, 284)

The virtual hallways of 2channel, then, are haunted not only by the ghostly narratives that are born and disseminated there but also by the inevitable decay that infects all spaces where human beings gather, tangible or not. In the same way that delivery technologies evolve to accommodate new forms of media transmission, so they evolve to accommodate new forms of haunting.

Kunekune is a classic 2channel ghost story, one that was born in the forums and spread from there to the larger Internet, and eventually even to a (very short and low-budget) film. The story apparently first appeared in the 2channel "Occult" message board in 2003, and while there are a few variations, the story has essentially remained the same since then (Kaidan News-b). A young boy returns to the countryside in Akita to visit his grandparents and goes for a walk with his brother. He notes that the air is cleaner than the air in the city, and that it's a hot day. Suddenly the wind stops, and the boy gets a bad feeling. His brother points across a field at something. Though there is no wind, the boy can faintly make out a figure, sort of like the white-clad body of a person, twisting around (*kunekune to ugokidashita*). Unnerved by the sight of the object moving when there is no wind, the boy's brother runs home to get some binoculars and looks through them. As soon as the brother looks through the binoculars, his face turns white. When the boy asks him what's wrong, the brother answers in a strange voice, "It's better if you don't know."

Before the boy can check the view from the binoculars, their grandfather comes running down the road and frantically asks the boy if he has looked through the binoculars at the white object yet. When the boy says "no," his grandfather looks relieved. They return to the house and the boy's brother appears to have lost his mind, laughing wildly and twisting on the floor just like the white object. The family decides to leave the brother in the countryside with the grandparents, and the boy weeps, because he feels that the person in front of him is no longer his brother, and never will be. Finally, perhaps in an effort to be closer to him, he sneaks a look at the white object through the binoculars. The final line of the story tells us "I saw, up close, the thing that I shouldn't have seen" (Matomedia 2013).

In addition to being a story of city people seeing something mysterious in the countryside, the story of *Kunekune* also shares another common feature of "electric tales"—it involves people looking at something that they should not look at, or discovering something that was better left unknown. A frequent warning attached to stories on the 2channel "Occult" message board is some version of "please do *not* look" (*zettai ni minai de kudasai*), which of course makes many people more likely to look. Just looking at the thing in question—or in some cases, hearing the forbidden story—will cause one to be cursed, sometimes with death, sometimes with madness. The story of "Tomino's Hell" holds that anyone who reads a certain poem out loud will be cursed, which led to numerous videos of people reading the poem being posted on 2channel—some people said that nothing happened, but others seemingly vanished after posting their videos, leading others to speculate that they had been cursed. The famous "red room" curse, a version of which is depicted in one of the feature films in the *2channel Curse* series, involves a mysterious pop-up that appears on your computer screen, which eventually leads you to a list of names, with your own name at the bottom—seeing it means that you will die tomorrow. And though not technically an "electric tale," one of Japan's most famous ghost stories, the story of the cursed videotape in *Ringu*, imagines that just watching a video will curse you with death in seven days (unless you copy the video and show it to someone else).

The idea of knowing that you will be cursed for looking at something but still not being able to resist looking at it is a particularly potent ghost story for the digital age, when we are constantly bombarded by "clickbait" and headlines that entice us by telling us *not* to look, or graphic images from news headlines that become even more intriguing when covered with a distortion filter and a warning about graphic imagery. Before the Internet and social media made almost all information easily accessible, urban legends relied on a lack of concrete information to maintain their air of mystery. Now, for those who would seek it out, there is no mystery—the origins and explanations of almost any "electric tale" can be easily found out. To keep up the allure, then, these stories have adapted, playing up the aspects of their narrative that are particularly intriguing for a generation raised online—the idea that you should not look at something, for example, or the idea that your own casual browsing habits will doom you.

The *Kunekune* story was made into a short, straight-to-video film in 2010 (directed by Kikkawa Hisatake). The story bore little resemblance to the original Internet story, effectively turning the monster into a version of Sadako from *Ringu*, a vengeful spirit in a white dress who curses everyone in the small community who sees her (after they had horrifically abused her for refusing to use her psychic powers to bring money to the town). Such a shift mirrors the way that films about Aokigahara, discussed in chapter 3, rely on the "realness" of the actual forest as a draw for the film, but ultimately present a story only tangentially related to well-known content produced about Aokigahara online. Still, the *Kunekune* movie maintains some elements of the story's "electric tale" flavor, making the protagonists a family from the city going camping in the countryside, a place that is immediately incomprehensible and forbidding (cell phones don't work, the car won't start, and the locals warn them to go back home). The DVD's product description on Amazon Japan also emphasizes the fact that it is a previously "unseen" story that has now been made "visible." Until now the story was shrouded in a "mysterious veil" (*nazo no bēru*), but now for the first time, it has been made into a movie (literally "visualized" / *eizō-ka*) (Amazon Japan 1996–2020). Ironically, though the description also mentions the story's origins on the Internet and 2channel specifically, what actually appears on screen bears very little resemblance to the original 2channel *Kunekune* story. What is "visualized" is effectively a hybrid of many different Japanese ghost stories and J-horror films, a story that bears little resemblance to the Internet-based *Kunekune* story that people might be familiar with.

As one of the first Japanese urban legends to be truly "born" on the Internet (rather than via word of mouth or mass media), *Kunekune* shows the influence of both its place of origin and the manner of its dissemination. It is short and relies on "scrolling" for optimum impact (ending with the idea of "seeing that which shouldn't have been seen"). To an audience of readers who are likely city dwellers, it also presents an idyllic and yet vaguely threatening image of the rural. And it plays with notions of "reality," presenting itself as a thing that actually happened (to someone's friend or classmate) even if its copy-paste existence on a more hoax-aware Internet all but guarantees that no one will actually end up fearful of white figures in fields. Experiencing it as a story online, viewed via a smartphone screen or computer screen, places it within a digital world that is already associated with the ghostly, while watching the film on a DVD or via streaming allows one to imagine that a previously "unseen" story is now being made visible.

The DVD and film series *2channel Curse* (*2channeru no noroi*, various directors, 2010-2013) collects stories from 2channel's "Occult" message board and presents them as a series of short films, as well as two feature-length films released in 2011 and 2012. Stories depicted in this series include *Kotoribako* (the story of a cursed box connected to the murder of children, also discussed in chapter 3); *Samejima jiken* (Samejima Incident), about an incident on a mysterious island that no one is supposed to talk about; the "red room" curse, about a computer popup image that curses anyone who sees it with death; and *Umigame sūpu* (Sea Turtle Soup), about a man who mysteriously dies by suicide after ordering sea turtle soup at a restaurant. What we usually see in these films are a mix of familiar ghost stories and a story of how the characters found out about the stories on 2channel. Characters are caught up in the ghost story, but they are also aware of 2channel as the place where the story originated or spread, with some characters occasionally expressing skepticism about whether anything on 2channel is accurate. There are frequent scenes of characters scrolling through threads on the 2channel "Occult" message board, messaging others for help on 2channel, or following instructions that they received on 2channel. 2channel text is often pictured red against a black screen, with ominous music playing in the background. Sometimes it isn't the ghost that is dangerous, it's 2channel itself, as when the site tells characters to quickly drink a glass of water to "purify" themselves after coming into contact with a ghost photograph—but then it turns out that drinking water while looking at certain text on the 2channel message boards has in fact cursed them. Standard stories of ghosts are thus mixed with frequent images of media devices and characters interacting with the Internet, often with deadly results.

The experience of watching *2channel Curse* at home on a computer mirrors Alexander Galloway's case study of Norman Rockwell's 1960 "Triple Self-Portrait," a painting of the artist painting himself in which we see the artist from the back, his reflection in a mirror, his painted (and more idealized) image on a canvas, several practice sketches pinned to the canvas, and other famous self-portrait images of European masters pinned to the other side of the canvas. In Rockwell's painting, Galloway argues, there is "a circulation of coherence . . . that gestures to the outside, while ultimately remaining afraid of it" (Galloway 2012, 34). In this "meditation on the interface itself" (34), our questions about the "line between text and paratext" make us realize that "an interface is not a thing; an interface is an effect . . . not media but mediation" (36). Viewing Rockwell's "Triple Self-Portrait" forces the viewer to acknowledge multiple frames and perspectives simultaneously, creating confusion about what is outside/inside the frame. Similarly, watching *2channel Curse* puts the viewer both inside and outside the frame of the films' stories. In my own experience, I watched many of the short films on my laptop on a desk, my smartphone nearby, framed photographs and clutter in the background. Watching one of these films on Amazon Prime Video, it appears as a single window on my computer screen, one of multiple tabs open on my Internet browser, my digital desktop clutter mirroring the more tangible clutter on my actual "desktop." Images from the films (in this case, a connecting thread from volume two that involves a young man alone in his apartment searching through the 2channel "Occult" message board) mirror the image that one might see of me from behind, in front of my own computer, watching the film (figure 1.1). And of course, should I choose to, I might, like the characters

Figure 1.1 Watching *2channel Curse* on a laptop. *Source*: Photo taken by author.

in the film, search the Internet (on my computer or nearby smartphone) for information about the stories I'm seeing depicted in the film. Multiple screens, multiple frames, and multiple perspectives—the line between text and paratext is eternally blurred. The stories not only point to something outside of the frame but also pull the outside *into* the film experience.

The short film *Webcam Call* (*Webbu kamera tsūwa*, dir. Nagae Jirō 2010), one of several short films collected in volume one of the *2channel Curse* series, clearly reveals these dizzying layers of perspective and mediation. The film opens with an image of a computer screen. Within that screen, there are four other small windows that show four people in four separate locations—a group of friends who have gathered for a modern *hyakumonogatari kaidankai*. In this version of the tradition, the four friends each sit in their own rooms in the dark, lit only by the light of their computer screens and a single candle that sits on their desks. From the beginning, only one character, Chika, is presented to us via "film camera"—everyone else is viewed only through the slightly grainy lens of their webcams. A frame (Chika's computer screen) within a frame (the *Webcam Call* short film), and four windows into four separate worlds within Chika's computer screen, all of them lit not only by the light of a candle but also by the equally ghostly light of a digital screen (figure 1.2).

Two of the characters tell short stories. One describes seeing a dark shadow of a woman in his webcam but looking back to see nothing—this story is

Circulating Urban Legends 39

Figure 1.2 Multiple windows and frames in *Webcam Call* (Nagae Jirō 2010). *Source*: Screenshot taken by author.

relayed to us via black-and-white images of the man, his webcam, and the ghostly reflection within it. This man blows out his candle after he finishes his story. Chika, for her part, cannot think of a story and says she will "go last," and then frantically asks for help from the "Occult" message board of 2channel. Before she can get a response, one of the other characters says: "My scary story . . . is that we all died in an accident yesterday" (Nagae 2010). Chika is horrified. Within the webcam image of herself on the computer screen, she sees a hand on her shoulder, but then sees nothing when she turns around. All of her friends' screens suddenly show only empty chairs and candles. A message on the 2channel thread she has been looking at tells her to click a link, where she sees a news story about three university students killed in a car crash, with one remaining in a coma. We then cut to a shot of her three friends behind her, their faces half-rotted. One says: "We're always together, huh?" (Nagae 2010). The final shot shows Chika in a hospital bed and the sound of a heart monitor flatlining.

The story is familiar in the world of urban legends—a group of people or a single person discovers that someone they encountered was actually a ghost.[5] But in the execution, we can see remarkable connections between old and new methods of storytelling and the ghostliness of the mediated image. The practice of *hyakumonogatari kaidankai* hails from the Edo period, but these characters are doing it via webcam. We, the viewers, watch the film of this event on our TV or computer screen (definitely not on a movie theater screen, because it was never released in theaters). Within that frame, we watch things unfold on Chika's laptop screen, the frame of which is visible in an early shot. Within *that* screen, we see four smaller "windows" into four smaller worlds—four people, each transmitting stories digitally, but presented in the manner of spoken word storytelling events, with candles burning beside them. Within Chika's webcam frame, we see ghostly images—of a hand, of a shadow behind someone—that don't appear in the "real" world. The image of empty chairs in the windows on Chika's computer screen is particularly eerie—such images already feel insubstantial, but the complete absence of other people makes the image more frightening. When the illusion ends for Chika, she finally sees her three friends as "real"—they stand behind her chair, not an image in a webcam, but actually there, presented to us via the film camera, their faces rotted and bloodied.

In addition to being a "meditation on the interface," *Webcam Call* beautifully illustrates the importance of frame-within-frame images in Japanese horror. Just as gradually extinguishing candles in a dark room during a night of ghost storytelling makes the atmosphere in the room grow more eerie, so the presence of multiple frames increases the sense of uncanniness for the viewer. Each frame/window increases the distance between the spectator and any sense of certainty about what is real and what is ghostly, while within the narrative the mixing of 2channel forum searches and storytelling styles that hail from the Edo period reveals the tension that always exists between older and newer forms of media.

Invented Urban Legends and Depictions of Old/New Media: *Toshimaen: The Movie*

Given that urban legends are by nature fictional, the idea of "invented" urban legends may seem to be a misnomer, but there are levels and degrees of invention. Films like *Carved: The Slit-Mouthed Woman* (*Kuchisake-onna*, dir. Shiraishi Kōji 2007), *Teketeke* (dir. Shiraishi Kōji 2009), and *Hanako-san of the Toilet* (*Toire no Hanako-san*, dir. Matsuoka Jōji 1995) are based on urban legends that were established in decades past through word of mouth and traditional media. Films like *Shirome* (discussed in chapter 2) and the more famous *Ringu*, though, present the idea that certain urban legends, like Sadako's cursed videocassette or the wish-granting god Shirome, have always existed, even though they were invented for the films in question (or, in the case of *Ringu*, for the novel that the film was based on). These films rely on the conventions of urban legends—the idea that many people have heard the story but are skeptical that it's true, and the faintly moralizing tone that often accompanies its consequences, for example. The paradox of creating a fictional version of something that is already inherently fictional further adds to the sense of fractured reality that these stories present.

The 2019 film *Toshimaen: The Movie* (*Eiga: Toshimaen*, dir. Takahashi Hiroshi)[6] is based on (and was filmed primarily on location at) the actual Toshimaen theme park in Tokyo's Nerima ward. Early on, we learn that there is a "Toshimaen curse" that involves many different actions and locations inside the park.[7] If you do any one of these actions, you will be pulled into a "secret space" and trapped there. The film follows a group of college-aged female friends on a last, nostalgic trip to the park. They initially joke about the curse but then begin disappearing one by one. In flashbacks, we learn that an absent girl, Yuka, was bullied by some of the other girls into knocking on an old building's door and that she has been trapped in the "secret space" of the park ever since.

Built in 1923 and shut down in 2020 to be replaced by a Harry Potter-themed park in 2023, Toshimaen was one of Japan's oldest theme parks (the oldest is Hanayashiki in Asakusa, which has been operating since 1853) (Taito City Culture Guide Archives 2019). Less flashy than the more modern (and more popular) Disneyland, Disney Sea, and Universal Studios theme parks, Toshimaen nonetheless invoked deep nostalgia for many older visitors. It was particularly well known for its merry-go-round, the Carousel El Dorado, which was built in Germany in 1907 and featured hand-carved wooden horses (Oricon News 2020). In addition to the difficulty of competing with Disney and Universal theme parks, however, by the time of its closure in 2020 Toshimaen's facilities had been showing their age for some time (*Mainichi Shinbun* 2020). The 2020 Toshimaen film seems to have been conceived at least partly as a last gasp promotion for the park. In the days leading up to Toshimaen's closure, the movie theater located near the theme park hosted a series of "countdown" screenings of the film (Eiga: Toshimaen 2020).

Toshimaen: The Movie, then, arrives already connected to a particular kind of nostalgia for "old" Japan and theme parks. This is reinforced in the film's narrative, which focuses on college student Saki getting ready to leave for a study abroad program in Australia. Her friends Anju, Chiaki, Ami, and Kaya suggest going to Toshimaen one last time after Saki receives free tickets from the mother of Yuka (the member of their group who mysteriously vanished at some point in the past). The girls discuss their fond memories of the park and look at pictures taken there in the past, including a paper photo given to Saki by Yuka's mother of the two of them as small children. In the same way that Saki is leaving childhood (and "old" Japan) behind to study in Australia, so the real Toshimaen is being dismantled to make way for a more "worldly" theme park. Though the entire film takes place within Tokyo, Toshimaen functions as the "rural" aspect of the urban-rural divide that is so common in "net lore," not only connected to a mythic version of childhood but also filled with strange and unknowable phenomena.

Where *Toshimaen: The Movie* truly reveals the "modern" evolution of the urban legend, though, is in both the film and its marketing campaign's juxtaposition of old and new media, which is woven seamlessly into the narrative. The film's poster shows a cracked smartphone held in a necrotic hand, the screen showing a cheerful photograph of the film's main characters at the park, blood spattered over the image. It appears as if they are trapped within the phone's screen, and this will play out in the film, when the "Toshimaen curse" effectively traps them all inside the park and within their own heavily mediated memories. The film opens, like so many Japanese horror films focused on urban legends or digital haunting, with the sound and image of a staticky screen, reminding the viewer of found-footage horror aesthetics. Rather than the specific image of TV "snow," though (an image that opens many of the *Ringu* sequels and other found footage-style Japanese horror films), this time the image more closely resembles a slightly blurry, pixelated online video. The first scene features a group of people filming a "spooky" video on the grounds of Toshimaen at night. The video is clearly streaming on Niconico, the Japanese video site that features real-time comments that scroll across the video itself (rather than appearing below it or off to the side). Marc Steinberg (2019) calls these comments the "most defining feature" of Niconico, noting that

> in the process of commenting, new contents are created . . . Comments write affective tonality and interpretive gestures into the fabric of the video itself . . . [The] comments are the source of innovation, media connection, and community formation, and the origin of a language shared by users about media that in turn informs media. (Steinberg 2019, 191)

By opening the film with this intimate form of video sharing and creation, *Toshimaen: The Movie* creates yet another layer of mediation that blurs the position of the viewer.

The three people in the video—Yucchi, Chamu, and Aiko—lay out the parameters of the "Toshimaen curse" as they film at night within the park. One: don't knock on the door of the old western-style building. Two: don't respond to anything you hear in the haunted house. And three: don't look in the "secret mirror" of the mirror house. If you do any of these things, you will be pulled into a "secret space" within the park.[8] The only way to escape the secret space is to ride the park's famous merry-go-round. In the beginning of the video, text comments scroll from right to left across the screen, variations on "Whoa!", "Creepy!" and "This is too much!" After Yucchi knocks on the door of the old western-style building, and Chamu is suddenly dragged inside, the text becomes thicker and moves more quickly. When Aiko and then Yucchi are dragged away by invisible forces, the text comments become long strings of a single hiragana symbol repeated ("Aaaaaahhhhh!", "Ohhhhhhhhh!"). Finally, as Yucchi screams in terror, the comments become a garbled mix of meaningless symbols and random characters, zigging and zagging chaotically all over the screen before disappearing completely (figure 1.3). The fallen camera then reveals the merry-go-round turning on by itself before the image cuts to the film's title, again presented with sounds of static and images of blurry pixels.

In *Toshimaen: The Movie* our gateway to a spooky story is a new media object—an amateur video produced for a platform that effectively turns the audience into an active part of the video production process. The streamed comments, most of them variations on "no, don't do it" and "this is scary," are a part of the video-viewing experience itself. Where platforms like YouTube place comments below the video, Niconico makes the comments an integral part of the video itself. (This will also be the case in the Niconico video that appears in *Sadako 3D*, discussed in chapter 4.) Importantly, in this first video image that opens the film, the perspective never shifts—from beginning to end, we view the video as if we were watching it on a computer or smartphone. Later, we will watch the group of friends at the center of *Toshimaen: The Movie* watch the video on their phones and see how it leads them to inadvertently create a malevolent force that will eventually claim all of them.

Toshimaen: The Movie includes repeated images of its main characters filming themselves, filming each other, and watching videos on their smartphones. The viewer's perspective frequently shifts between the smartphone's view of events and the film's view, and what the characters see is often misleading—a video taken of the window of Yuka's old house shows nothing, but the same video viewed later shows a ghostly image of Yuka, who then pops up in physical form behind the phone. Text messages and voice

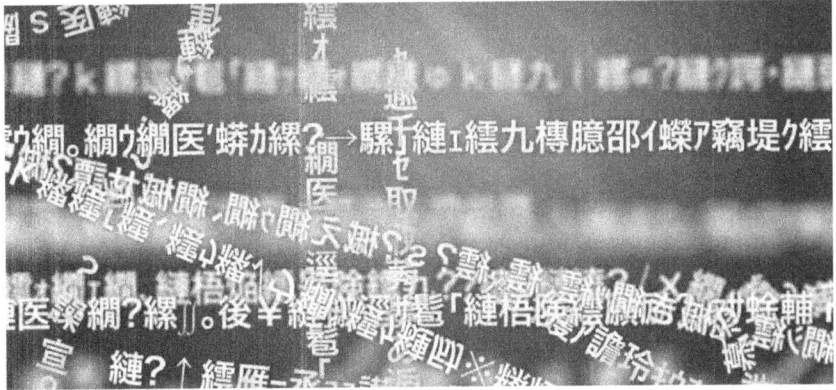

Figure 1.3 Comments scroll chaotically across the screen of a Niconico video in *Toshimaen: The Movie* (Takahashi Hiroshi 2019). *Source*: Screenshot taken by author.

messages lead the girls astray. In one scene, Chiaki films Anju standing in front of the old western-style building, talking about the curse in the same manner as the group from the beginning of the film. We see Chiaki's hands holding the phone, the video within the frame of the phone's screen, and also a slightly blurred image of the "real" events outside the phone frame, all at the same time. Then the perspective shifts so that the phone video fills the entire screen, complete with the timer and other in-screen buttons. Anju pulls Saki into the phone video frame and tells her to knock on the door. The perspective shifts to the "film" view as Saki hesitantly moves toward the door, but then shifts back to the phone camera view when Kaya suddenly rushes forward and knocks herself, scaring Saki. Though perspective doesn't shift back, we see that Chiaki is still filming. When a strange man opens the door, we again see a frame-within-frame perspective: Chiaki filming the strange man on her phone, and the film camera's view of the man, both within the same shot. All of these frame-within-frame shots underscore the extent to which the film is focused on mediated images and memories, and the extent to which the girls' sense of reality—particularly their sense of reality concerning their relationship to Yuka, and how badly they treated her—is dependent on their literal and figurative frames of reference.

Like so many films associated with urban legends, *Toshimaen: The Movie* exists as a kind of cautionary tale, presenting new media technologies and devices as damaging to young people's lives in a way that older media is not. Japanese horror narratives, particularly those centered around different forms of media, have always been connected to feelings of uneasiness surrounding all kinds of old and new media. The original *Ringu*, with its deadly images transmitted via videotape and its warped photographs, "associates ubiquitous technological mediation—that is, the cameras, televisions sets, videocassette recorders, telephones and other such hardware foregrounded throughout the film—with the intrusion of 'posthuman' otherness into contemporary cultural life" (White 2005, 41). *Ringu* illustrates "not only the parallels between occult and technological media, as spectral images and voices repeatedly manifest themselves through media technologies, but also the threat that these technologies pose to the integrity and autonomy of the subject" (Enns 2010, 31). Citing Konaka Chiaki's "Konaka theory" of horror and Takahashi Hiroshi's film criticism on the representation of ghosts, Kinoshita (2009) places J-horror discourse "within a long tradition of film theory that shows particular fascination with the photo-based film's ability to render the living and the dead, the human and the ghost, and the animate and the inanimate indiscernible" (Kinoshita 2009, 114). Konaka and Takahashi agree that "the ghost's voice is most scary when mediated through technology of mechanical reproduction such as recording and broadcasting" (Konaka 2003, 114–115, quoted in Kinoshita 2009, 115). While not so much a simplistic collection of "media is bad" narratives, films like *Pulse* and *Ringu* do focus on the way that certain media technologies blur the line between living and dead, tangible and intangible.

Similarly, *Toshimaen: The Movie*'s focus on Niconico videos and smartphone recordings reveals both the ubiquity of these technologies and the way that they can often undermine our sense of what is real or certain. Additionally, "old" media (in the form of paper photos) is often depicted as something innocent and good, while "new" media (in the form of Niconico videos, smart phones, and smart phone videos) is sinister and connected to bullying. In the beginning of the film, Yuka's mother tries to give Saki a paper photo of the two girls as small children, but Saki rejects it out of guilt (we later learn that Saki also played a part in the bullying that led to Yuka's disappearance). Later, the photo turns up mysteriously bloodied in Saki's bag. On Saki's wall are paper photos of all the girls together, smiling and making peace signs at the camera. When we see the girls engaging with "new" media, though, it's usually in a negative way—they film each other knocking on the door of Yuka's abandoned house as a joke, they gawk at the Niconico video about the Toshimaen curse as a way to bully Yuka, they receive misleading text messages or videos from malevolent spirits on their phones, and Yuka's filming of herself knocking on the door of an old building inside the park is what leads to her disappearance. New media, it seems, leads to fractured relationships and self-centeredness, where old media (especially print media) is associated with a more innocent time.

In both its narrative and its creation/marketing, then, *Toshimaen: The Movie* represents nostalgia for old media and entertainment forms as well as the ubiquity of new media forms. It centers on a real space suffused with nostalgia that at the time of the film's release was soon to be destroyed, making the film itself into a kind of haunted relic. Within the film's narrative, nostalgia is experienced both through the park itself and the faded paper photos that the group of female friends share with each other, while uneasiness and eeriness come via newer media technologies like Niconico videos and smartphone recordings. As the image on the DVD cover shows, this piece of the modern Japanese horror film landscape sees young women literally trapped within the cracked, bloody frame of a smartphone screen, death lurking just beyond the boundaries of that frame in the form of a vengeful spirit that has made its way from the world of Internet urban legends into their "real" world.

CONCLUSION

Whether shared around a campfire with a group of children, through frightening paintings exhibited in a temple, by clicking on threads on an Internet forum, or attending a live telling of traditional ghost stories by lantern light, ghost stories, and their telling endure, even if the manner of their telling and dissemination changes with the advent of new technologies. Via films like the *2channel Curse* series, we can see how computers, smartphones, and platforms like 2channel have embedded themselves into the presentation of the stories via film, resulting in a final product that is both *about* the technology and disseminated *through* it (for those who watch the films on their laptops, tablets, or smartphones). In a film like *Toshimaen: The Movie*, we enter the world of the film via a Niconico video with its rapidly streaming, real-time comments, putting us in the position of a viewer who came across this video online. Later, our perspective shifts constantly between the film itself and the smartphone videos that the characters are watching or filming, our view framed by the borders of their new media devices. Like Rockwell's "Triple Self-Portrait," all of this framing-within-framing shows us the "thin line between text and paratext" (Galloway) and reminds us of how "the frame positions the viewer" (Friedberg) . . . or leaves the viewer eternally uncertain as to their position. In our interactions with Japanese ghost stories in the digital age, we must reckon not only with the age-old specters that haunt the characters within the stories but also with the strange uncertainty of our own place within the narrative and the film viewing experience.

NOTES

1. 2channel's structure of image posting and anonymous commenting divided into "threads" of a limited number inspired the creation of similar sites like 4chan and Reddit (both of which have faced similar problems regarding harassment and hate speech). The original 2channel site, founded by Nishimura Hiroyuki, was taken over by N.T. Technology chairman Jim Watkins in 2014. Nishimura then created a competing site called 2ch.sc, while Watkins eventually renamed the original 2channel to 5channel to avoid legal issues (Akimoto 2014, Robertson 2015). Since 2014 traffic has been divided between the two sites, though it would appear that 5channel receives considerably more traffic, based on data compiled by each website (Tōkō-sū tōkei@ 2ch keijiban 2021; SPARROW AIM-7P 2021). To further confuse matters, in 2015 Nishimura bought and became the administrator of 4chan, the U.S.-based website arguably inspired by 2channel (Akimoto 2014, Robertson 2015).

2. *Train Man* (*Densha otoko*) refers to a supposedly authentic 2004 2channel thread that became a book, manga, TV series, and movie. In the thread, a self-identified *otaku* who was dubbed "Train Man" claimed that he had protected a woman from a drunk on a train, and that the woman had then sent him an expensive gift as a thank you. "Train Man" sought advice from other 2channel users on how to woo the woman, and the two ended up dating. For more, see Alisa Freedman's 2009 essay "*Train Man* and the Gender Politics of Japanese '*Otaku*' Culture: The Rise of New Media, Nerd Heroes and Consumer Communities," and Susan Napier's

2011 chapter "Where Have All the Salarymen Gone? Masculinity, Masochism, and Technomobility in *Densha Otoko*," in *Recreating Japanese Men*, edited by Sabine Frühstück and Anne Walthall.

3. In English-language media, stories like these are often referred to as "creepypasta," a term that originated on the 4chan message boards and was taken from "copy-paste." The name refers to the fact that these stories are copied and pasted from different sites around the Internet. Today, many of these stories are collected at creepypasta.com and the NoSleep subreddit.

4. Maekawa (2015) argues that *toshidensetsu* does not have quite the same meaning as "urban legend." As introduced in Japan in the 1980s, the word distinguished itself from "folk tales" (*minwa*) of the past in that urban legends were stories spread primarily through the frame of media (rather than orally). Other important features of *toshidensetsu* are that they have more of a sense of "fragmentation" (*danpensei*) than other stories and do not always have a clear point of origin (16).

5. One of the more famous examples of this story is the "vanishing hitchhiker," documented by Jan Harold Brunvand (2003). In various versions of this story, someone picks up a hitchhiker who later vanishes from the car, and the driver learns that the person died a long time ago. Variations of this story also appeared in Tōhoku after the 2011 quake and tsunami, with taxi drivers claiming that they picked up passengers who then vanished (Pereira 2016).

6. As mentioned in the introduction, the director of *Toshimaen: The Movie* and the screenwriter of *Don't Look Up* and *Ringu* are both named Takahashi Hiroshi, but are different people (their first names are written with different kanji).

7. While there are a variety of urban legends related to Japanese amusement parks (particularly Tokyo Disneyland), the particular actions that lead to the "Toshimaen curse" appear to have been invented for *Toshimaen: The Movie*.

8. Another urban legend that involves being pulled into another dimension is the "elevator game," which some claim originated on the 2channel "Occult" message board (though others claim that the story began in Korea). Supposedly, pushing a series of buttons in an elevator and exiting on a certain floor will leave the player in another dimension, and the only way to escape is to push the buttons again in a certain order when you return to the elevator (Gray 2020).

Chapter 2

Idols, Japanese Horror, and Fractured Realities
Shirome

As we have seen, the sharing of scary stories and urban legends frequently moves between different media platforms and devices, though in the 2010s and beyond such sharing has taken place largely on the Internet. Many of these stories rely on a semblance of reality and authenticity to achieve their desired effects—though readers on 2channel likely know that what they are reading is fiction, these stories are presented and engaged with as if they really happened. Whether consumed via a feature film or an online post, such stories use the *appearance* of realness to generate fear and discomfort. Films like *Toshimaen: The Movie* and the short films collected in *2channel Curse* also take many of their aesthetic and structural cues from the found-footage horror genre, making use of simple camera work, editing, and lighting that make the films look slightly unpolished, or mixing amateur YouTube and Niconico videos in with the film itself. That mix of amateur/professional quality and film/online video aesthetics further blurs the line between reality and fiction.

In this chapter, I will examine how notions of reality and authenticity are "fractured" in the Japanese found-footage horror film *Shirome* (dir. Shiraishi Kōji 2010), one of many Japanese (found-footage) horror films to feature Japanese pop stars known as "idols." *Shirome* stars Momoiro Clover Z, an idol group composed of six girls between the ages of thirteen and sixteen. In the film, the girls, playing versions of themselves, are purportedly being filmed for an extended TV show segment on ghost stories. They are told of a wish-granting spirit called Shirome that resides in an abandoned school. (As in *Toshimaen: The Movie*, the "urban legend" of Shirome was invented for the film, though it is presented as if it is widely known.) If the girls want to achieve their dream of appearing on the annual Kōhaku Uta-Gassen singing competition show, they need to travel to the school to express their wishes to

Shirome. But if anything in their wish is deemed "impure," they are warned, they will be dragged into hell.

"Idol horror" films, beyond being promotional vehicles for their stars, often reveal the constant tension that exists between authenticity and illusion in the worlds of both found-footage horror and Japanese idol culture, as well as how that sense of authenticity is further complicated by an endless array of media objects and devices. Both the idol world and the found-footage horror world are predicated on a kind of "mutual agreement" between audience and subject—namely, that the subjects will present something that has the appearance of realness and authenticity (genuine-seeming emotion and affection from the idols, a documentary-style realness from the horror film). At the same time, the audiences for both the film and the idol performance will suspend a certain amount of disbelief, aware that what they are seeing is fiction but deriving pleasure through engaging from it as if it were fact. The idol horror film can also serve as one component of a "database" (Azuma 2009), a small component of a larger whole that is easily consumed by an idol fan.

Since the release of the 1988 film *Psychic Vision* (*Jaganrei*, dir. Ishii Teruyoshi), "idol horror" films have also frequently depicted the inherent spectrality of cinema and photography, connecting the constant photographing and videotaping of idols with stories of haunted celluloid, cursed videos, and *shinrei shashin* (ghost photography). Seen through a mix of POVs, frames, and media devices, the collections of "found" footage that make up the narratives in these films draw our attention not only to what is visible but also to what is invisible or blurred. Ultimately, *Shirome* reveals the "spatially and temporally fractured frames" (Friedberg 2006, 7) through which spectators connect to the worlds of both Japanese found-footage horror and the Japanese idol.

JAPANESE IDOLS: MUTUAL AGREEMENTS, DATABASE CONSUMPTION, AND PERFORMING AUTHENTICITY

As they have existed in Japan since the 1980s, idols are very specific types of pop stars. They are typically young, single women who sometimes perform in groups and sometimes alone. They are petite and conventionally attractive, but are often described as having a somewhat "average" appearance rather than model/movie star looks, allowing them to seems like "everyday" people. Though technically they may be singers, they are not particularly skilled—they are celebrated more for their cheerful personalities and can-do attitudes. They usually dress somewhat conservatively and present an image of availability, though most eventually "graduate" from their idol careers and date, marry, and have children, transitioning into a more "adult" role. The parameters of the idol image became more specific in the 1980s, the "golden age of idols," a period when pop idols like "cutesy" Matsuda Seiko dominated the music scene (Galbraith and Karlin 2012, 4–5). Kitajima Yoshimasa notes that this was the period during which idols became less 'real' and more about performative cuteness:

> Seiko's popularity was only established upon viewers' understanding that an idol is nothing more than a 'doll' in television-land. In other words, fans loved Seiko with a more 'sophisticated' gaze than before, and her apparently fake acting which previously would probably have been rejected as 'phony-smelling' was now accepted as a 'mutual agreement (*o-yakusoku*)' with the audience in the realm of television. (Kitajima 2012, 152)

This mutual agreement—the idea that the pop idols will work hard to maintain certain illusions of availability, purity, and femininity, and that fans will buy into the illusion—has long been a feature of the idol-fan relationship.

Breaking this illusion can have severe consequences. In 2013, a widely circulated idol image both inside and outside Japan was a video of a shaven-headed young girl crying in front of a camera. The girl in the video was then-twenty-year-old Minegishi Minami, a member of the popular idol group AKB48. She spoke haltingly, tears streaming down her face, and apologized for "causing so much trouble" to her fans. Minegishi was apologizing for spending the night with her boyfriend, which violated the "no dating" clause of her AKB48 contract (and an unwritten rule for most female idols) (*BBC News* 2013). Watching the video (which was removed not long after it was posted), the most striking aspect was its seeming authenticity. Though it is highly likely that Minegishi's appearance in the video—like every other detail of her life as an AKB48 performer—was very carefully scripted and staged, her emotion felt raw, and her tears certainly looked real. We were, ostensibly, getting a peek behind a very thick curtain—seeing a moment of spontaneity in a world where raw displays of feeling are usually a performance. And yet the very notions of reality, authenticity, and spontaneity, already so slippery in any mediated image, are even more so in the world of idol culture. We cannot trust what we see, even when it triggers an emotional response that feels "real."

The endless manipulation and circulation of idol images is part of a contemporary media landscape in which we regularly consume massive amounts of information via a variety of screens. Baudrillard wrote of the "excess of information" that dominated daily life in the 1980s, while Friedberg noted in the early 2000s that a variety of screens further exacerbated our sense of being overwhelmed by information (Baudrillard 2016 [1985]; Friedberg 2006).

Spectacle had long been a dominant force in everyday life, "the sun which never sets over the empire of modern passivity" (Debord 1995 [1967], 13). In a world dominated by such spectacle and an excess of information, many turn to fictional worlds and narratives as a source of meaning, inhabiting a "forest of narrativities" that "organize in advance our work, our celebrations, and even our dreams" (de Certeau 1984, 186). As Ōtsuka Eiji has argued, for many self-identified *otaku* (many of whom are devoted fans of idol groups like Momoiro Clover Z), images, videos, and stories about fictional characters and idols exist as "small narratives" that fans can collect and reorganize to gain access to a "grand narrative." The idol is just one of those "small narratives," and Ōtsuka argues that the idol industry has convinced fans that "through the repetition of this very act of consumption they grow closer to the totality of the grand narrative," and thus "the sales of countless quantities of the same kind of commodity become possible" (Ōtsuka 2010, 107).

This tendency often plays out in the way that idol groups are marketed. The idol group AKB48, for example, holds annual elections for the most popular members. Each CD purchased includes a ballot, or in some cases, a chance to participate in a live meet-and-greet session. The CD is less valuable than the ballot or the ticket to the meet-and-greet, and fans often throw away the CD after purchasing it. Ōtsuka describes a similar practice among children who collected stickers featuring images of certain characters produced by Bikkuriman Chocolates in the 1980s—the children, who were eager to collect images of the many different characters depicted on the stickers, would throw the chocolates away and keep the stickers (Ōtsuka 2010, 106). Similarly, AKB48 fans may buy multiple copies of the same CD but throw most of the CDs away. What they are really purchasing is a ticket that gives them a stronger connection to (and control over) the group, and arguably a stronger connection to the narrative universe that the idols inhabit. This sort of behavior is further encouraged in games like *The Idolmaster*, where players manage a group of idols and try to make stars of them (Black 2012).

For Azuma Hiroki, though (drawing on Lyotard and *The Postmodern Condition*), a key feature of the postmodern world is the death of "grand narratives." Instead of "narrative consumption," otaku now engage in "database consumption," with fans focusing more on particular characters or tropes (small narratives) instead of a larger grand narrative (Azuma 2009). Azuma uses the example of Di Gi Charat, a female character created as a mascot for a dealer in anime and gaming-related products that, due to its popularity, ended up *inspiring* novels and anime, and thus its own "world." For otaku, to consume Di Gi Charat "is not simply to consume a work (a small narrative) or a worldview behind it (a grand narrative), nor to consume characters and settings (a grand nonnarrative). Rather, it is linked to consuming the database of otaku culture as a whole" (Azuma 2009, 54). I would argue that in the world of idol horror, there is a connection between both the small narrative (of an individual idol or a film like *Shirome*) and a larger world (of idol culture). If a film like *Shirome* and its images of idols serve as a component part, the larger world of idols and the pieces of that world that circulate via television, films, and the Internet—which include live performances, TV appearances, meet-and-greets, the idols' presentation of their personal lives, and tangible goods such as posters, clothing, and CDS—are the "grand narrative" (or grand non-narrative) that fans want to be connected to. Idol horror films are yet another component part of a vast universe of idol commodities, with the image of the idol in peril (and the feeling of protectiveness that comes from watching the idols in peril) serving as a means to bring the fan closer to the idol and to the larger world that they are a part of.

Idols and components of idol culture are easily transferred between platforms and different types of media at least partially because of their lack of uniqueness and "everyday" personalities. Idols are often seen as "authentic" for their relative lack of talent (or at least the sense that they are "works in progress" rather than polished professionals).[1] Importantly, an idol's lack of singing and dancing talent is actually a part of their appeal.[2] W. David Marx notes that a "bland" idol is ideal for the kind of cross-media performances and promotion that are often expected of idol performers—uniqueness is a detriment, not an advantage. Being only marginally talented as a performer is fine, but idols cannot be "controversial, unattractive, or disruptive" (Marx 2012, 51). An idol's existence as an easily transferable commodity is similar to that of both a *tarento*[3] and a film star, a "standardised product which (film producers) can understand, which can be advertised and sold, and which not only they, but also banks and exhibitors, regard as insurance for large profits" (Powdermaker 2013 [1950], 228–229, quoted in Dyer 1979, 11). An idol's less-than-stellar performing skills also give fans a chance to be "supporters" of the idol's journey from awkward newbie to polished professional. Galbraith and Karlin (2020) note that an idol's "roughness" (*dekoboko*) is what sets them apart from professional pop stars (56). AKB48 members are "average but more 'real,' whereas professional artists are spectacular but 'inhuman'" (Attwood 2007, 449, quoted in Galbraith and Karlin 2020, 57). Thus being less competent may be desirable for an idol. Idols' lack of uniqueness and easy transferability between different types of media further serves their purpose as components of a database, circulated for easy consumption.

Japanese pop idols might be characterized as fake or prepackaged in the same way as pop stars from other countries, whose image and musical sound have usually been carefully molded by production companies to appeal to the largest possible group of people. Like classic film stars, an idol's personality, fashion sense, and origin story are carefully crafted and disseminated. Everything that Japanese pop idols do in public is carefully planned—the clothes they wear, what they say in interviews, where they go, and what they do in their free time. At the same time, the creation of idol personae is likely not an entirely one-sided story of Svengali-like producers carefully shaping and molding young women for maximum appeal. Idols do play a role in their own image-making, particularly "underground" or lesser-known idols (as documentaries like *Tokyo Idols* [dir. Miyake Kyōko 2017] reveal), and while some of their emotions (particularly tears) may be exaggerated for the camera, the line between truth and performance can often be difficult to see. As Yu (2017) notes, "stardom has always functioned as a masquerade, and stars have been actively participating in the making of their own image from the beginning, albeit to various extents" (Yu 2017, 3).

Spontaneity is rare in the idol world (and not even necessarily desired by fans, who seek a particular version of femininity and purity that takes a great deal of rehearsal and polishing to maintain). In Stephanie Choi's work on the "intimate labor" of K-pop idols and fans, she describes how one of her informants used to work for an agency that employed one of her favorite K-pop idols, but eventually quit the job because it was unpleasant for her to see the idol when he wasn't "on" (when he was simply walking around the office and looking tired or bored) (Choi 2018). For this fan, at least, seeing an idol's "everyday" self was not desirable, and for many Japanese idol fans, maintaining the "mutual agreement" that allows the fan to believe that the idol is eternally cheerful, available, and devoted to fans is preferable to getting a glimpse of their "everyday" self.

The question of reality/authenticity and pop idols becomes even more complicated when one considers that Hatsune Miku, a pop star who regularly sells out large arenas in Japan, is a digital hologram. And in 2011, chocolate company Glico featured "Eguchi Aimi," a computer-generated composite image of multiple AKB48 members' faces, in a commercial. "Eguchi" had a profile on the group's website and had done a photo shoot, but fans were suspicious (not because "Eguchi" looked fake, but because she was appearing in a national commercial while still a trainee [*kenkyūsei*] in the group). Many defended her humanity online until Glico finally revealed that she was a composite image (Galbraith and Karlin 2012, 193). Though shocked, fans did not seem particularly put off by the deception, and in 2013, Eguchi officially "graduated" from AKB48. Fans expressed disappointment that she was gone from the official AKB48 site, with one calling her the "perfect idol" (*RBB Today* 2013). If fans are tacitly aware that the objects of their obsession traffic in illusion, the Eguchi Aimi stunt likely feels less like a trick and more like an extension of what AKB48 already is.

The Eguchi incident involved literally piecing together other AKB48 members' lips, eyes, cheeks, and eyebrows to create a virtual person. Widely circulated images and videos (some created by Glico itself), many of them disseminated online, reveal how pieces of several members' faces were captured on video and then combined to create "Eguchi," who was arguably quite convincing as a "real" person in the brief commercial (in any other context, viewers probably would not have recognized that she was a composite image) (figure 2.1). The process vividly illustrates the way that engagement with idols is often about collecting the pieces to make the whole—or, in the case of "database consumption," simply focusing on the pieces.

Such a layering of images that produces a "definitive uncertainty about reality" (Baudrillard 2016 [1985], 517) might be unsettling to some, but for many AKB48 fans (and perhaps for fans of hologram idols like Hatsune Miku), Eguchi Aimi represents everything that is desirable about the idol: not so much a *person*, she is more an easily manipulated image, one that can be fractured, re-formed, and easily circulated. She is a "'doll'" that fans view with a more "sophisticated gaze" (Kitajima 2012, 152), acknowledging her status as a digital composite but not necessarily seeing this as a betrayal of what the idol stands for. She is a component part of a larger whole that can be "collected" by fans who want access to a larger narrative universe, or simply enjoyed on its own, as a small narrative. Within the context of the Japanese horror films that they star in, the idol image can also be endlessly manipulated for the enjoyment of fans.

Fiction, reality, spectacle, and the endless circulation of images and stories—all of these aspects of idol culture happen via a number of screens and devices that have always offered a mediated version of "truth." The frames through which we view both the physical and the digital world—physical

Figure 2.1 "Eguchi Aimi" appears in a Glico commercial. *Source*: Screenshot taken by author.

windows, movie, and TV screens—alter what they reveal. Going back as far as the camera obscura and Leon Battista Alberti's fifteenth-century writings on painting, Anne Friedberg argues that for Alberti, a painting within a frame "was not intended to copy a literal view out the window but to recreate a spatial reconstruction of such a view" (Friedberg 2006, 30) while the camera obscura delighted viewers "due not to its verisimilitude, but to the *illusion* of verisimilitude" (Friedberg 2006, 60). In the 2010s and beyond, Japanese found-footage horror films featuring idols present their narratives via mini camcorders, portable DVD players, cell phone cameras, TV screens, computer screens, and more professional camera and sound equipment (nonetheless often edited to appear amateur). As we will see, all of these frames and the constant movement between them, as well as the frequent presence of media devices themselves within the film, constantly force the viewer to re-examine their own perspective and their sense of what is "real" or authentic within the film.

IDOLS AND FOUND-FOOTAGE HORROR

In the same way that the world of pop idols invites questions about authenticity, illusion, and "mutual agreements," found-footage horror films also force viewers to question their sense of what is real, and to what extent "reality" is manipulated through different media objects and devices. The genre can be loosely defined as a film that presents itself as either a documentary or a collection of unedited "found" camera footage, often connected to ghosts, the supernatural, monsters, or violence. Actors in found-footage horror films often seem to be improvising their lines and blocking, and shaky, unprofessional-looking camera work makes it appear that one of the actors, not a professional cameraperson, is filming everything. Though the form arguably extends as far back as Orson Welles' 1938 radio broadcast of *War of the Worlds*, it has firmly established its hold in the film industry in the years since the success of *The Blair Witch Project* (dir. Daniel Myrick and Eduardo Sánchez 1999). *Blair Witch* in particular, released at a time when only a small percentage of the population used the Internet, was arguably the first film to utilize "viral" or "guerrilla" marketing, spreading information about the film through a website, a supplementary TV special, bootleg videos, and an e-mail newsletter (Bereznak 2019). Photos and video clips were presented as "evidence" in a mystery that audiences could help solve. In those early days of found-footage horror, there was still a sense that this all might have actually happened.

Though the mockumentary and found-footage formats have certainly been used in genres other than horror, found-footage films specifically seem to gravitate toward the horror genre. Beyond *Blair Witch*, other representative examples include *Rec* (dir. Jaume Balagueró and Paco Plaza 2007), in which reporters covering a story end up trapped in a building with zombie-like monsters; *Paranormal Activity* (dir. Oren Peli 2007), in which a couple documents supernatural happenings in their home; and *Willow Creek* (dir. Bobcat Goldthwait 2013), in which a couple making a Bigfoot documentary in the woods get more than they bargained for. *Blair Witch* and its successors in the found-footage genre quickly established a familiar structure and aesthetic. "Actors" frequently played themselves and often used their own names. Cameras shook and wandered in and out of focus. Elements of the production process that would normally be edited out—heavy breathing into a microphone, wind sounds, camera buttons being turned on and off—were left in, further blurring the line between fiction and nonfiction. Fear often came from what we did *not* see, or expecting to see something frightening that never emerged. Endings were abrupt, often with a brief bit of text that mentioned the circumstances under which the footage was found.

All of the "messiness" of these films added to the feelings of authenticity, and by extension the fear. In perhaps the most famous shot from *Blair Witch*, protagonist Heather films herself weeping in extreme close-up, tears, and snot running down her face. The scene has become a joke, but at the time of *Blair Witch*'s release, I recall it being one of the rawest expressions of terror and grief I had ever seen on film. (Minegishi Minami's apology video has a similar effect—we are ostensibly seeing the "messy" version of her, and the video is deeply affecting because it feels so intimate.) In *Paranormal Activity*, much of the discomfort comes from watching a couple's relationship unravel in real time as they struggle to deal with malevolent supernatural forces in their home. At one point the man, Mika, drops the camera that he is always holding and crouches down to comfort his girlfriend Katie, who is sobbing, curled up on the floor. We hear her sobs and his comforting words but see only a fraction of their bodies within the frame. Here, too, the scene is affecting because of its seeming lack of artifice—we are supposedly seeing how people behave when they are not being filmed (even though the camera is still there).

Much of the effectiveness of found-footage horror comes down to careful editing, framing, and camera movement, all of which is designed to appear accidental (or at least to exist as "raw" and undoctored footage) but is in fact a collection of carefully chosen footage, not simply "found," as the genre would indicate. Director Shiraishi Kōji argues that the "reality" of found-footage films (what he often calls "fake documentary") is actually created through editing: "Editing in fake documentaries is much more important than in regular dramas. Editing is connected to the world of the film, and if you don't connect the reality of the film and the editing, the film's world won't be established" (Shiraishi 2016, 140). What the filmmaker edits, Shiraishi argues, is what the spectator sees, and what the spectator sees constitutes the reality of the film (140). Screenwriter Konaka Chiaki echoes this in his discussion of the "fundamentals" of J-horror, arguing that it is not so much about presenting a "real thing" (*hontō no koto*) but something that *looks* like a real thing (*hontō ni mieru koto*) (Konaka 2003, 141). "Pseudo-documentary" films, Konaka argues, are "enigmatic material" that exist in the space between fiction and reality (141). The most fundamental type of fear is created when various technical and narrative elements combine organically to create a true "in-story reality" (145). What we see on the screen, though it works to appear as a "found" media object, is in fact the result of careful choices that create a particular version of reality.

Where early found-footage films like *Blair Witch* and *Cannibal Holocaust* (dir. Ruggero Deodato 1980) played up the question of whether the footage and the events depicted were real, by now found-footage horror operates under a "mutual agreement" principle similar to that between idol and idol fan: the filmmakers work hard to create a realistic environment, and the spectators temporarily accept it. Additionally, as Alexandra Heller-Nicholas writes, certain aesthetic characteristics of found-footage horror—shaky camera work, awkward lighting, intertitles, and sudden cuts, all of which appear in *Shirome*—are now less an indicator of "realness" than of genre (Heller-Nicholas 2014, 8). Where once these aesthetic choices indicated authenticity, now they indicate that we are watching a very specific type of horror film. Films like *Cloverfield* (dir. Matt Reeves 2008), an alien invasion story made with a much larger budget than a typical found-footage horror film, have even adopted the cheap/amateur aesthetic to lend an air of authenticity to the "found footage" aspect of their stories. Audiences who watched *Blair Witch* successors like *Rec*, *Paranormal Activity*, and *Willow Creek* were much savvier, media-wise, than those who first watched *Blair Witch*. But the pleasure in watching found footage still arguably comes from the same place: from engaging with a story *as if* it were real. The continued presence of these moments meant to convince us we are watching "amateur" (and therefor authentic) footage—dropped or shaky cameras, the beeps and clicks of camera equipment, poorly framed shots—keeps the illusion convincing enough that audiences can still experience the fear and catharsis that comes from watching "real" frightening events on screen.

Though some of the most famous examples of classic J-horror are not found-footage horror, as Zahlten and Brown have noted, J-horror arguably owes much of its aesthetic to mockumentary-style series like *True Scary Stories* (*Hontō ni atta kowai hanashi*) (Zahlten 2017, 163; Brown 2018, 2). Japan also has a long history of sharing "true" scary stories in various media forms, from the *School Ghost Stories* (*Gakkō no kaidan*) series of books and films to TV segments and programs like *True Scary Stories* that focus on "things that really happened." Though Nakata Hideo's *Don't Look Up* and *Ringu* are generally regarded as the origin point of J-horror, Kinoshita Chika notes that another possible point of origin is Ishii Teruyoshi's 1988 film *Psychic Vision*, which is in fact a found-footage horror film (Kinoshita 2009, 235 n.31). Looking at Japanese found-footage horror films from the late 2000s and beyond, we can see both the influence of this domestic tradition and elements imported from English-language found-footage horror films. *Paranormal Activity: Tokyo Night* (*Paranōmaru akutibiti dai ni shō: Tōkyō naito*, dir. Nagae Toshikazu 2010) follows a story similar to *Paranormal Activity*, with a young man using a camera to document strange happenings in the home he shares with his sister. *POV: A Cursed Film* (*POV: Norowareta firumu*, dir. Tsuruta Norio 2012) focuses on a TV shoot involving two young actresses that takes a dark turn when they accidentally watch a ghostly video. While not entirely a found-footage horror film, *Hide and Seek Alone* (*Hitori kakurenbō*, dir. Yamada Masafumi 2009) features many scenes shot on handheld cameras by its performers, who are spending the night filming in a school in the hopes of contacting the dead.

Shirome director Shiraishi Kōji is perhaps the most prolific found-footage horror filmmaker in Japan, though his career as a screenwriter, film director, and TV director includes a wide range of horror types—the *Ringu* and *Grudge* crossover *Sadako vs. Kayako* (2016), the ultraviolent, banned-in-the-UK splatter film *Grotesque* (*Gurotesuku*, 2009); *Carved: The Slit-Mouthed Woman* (*Kuchisake-onna*, 2007), a retelling of the slit-mouthed woman urban legend; and the *Files of Mystery and Dread: Too Scary* (*Senritsu kaiki fairu: Kowasugi*, 2012–2015) series. A recurring theme and style, though, is the "true ghost story," often framed as a form of found footage or mockumentary that frequently stars the director himself. Included in this group of films are *The Curse* (*Noroi*, 2005), about a filmmaker who disappeared while making a documentary about an ancient demon; *Occult* (*Okaruto*, 2009), which sees Shiraishi playing a version of himself trying to document the existence of paranormal phenomena; and *Cursed Violent People* (*Bachiatari bōryoku ningen*, 2010a), in which two violent thugs bully Shiraishi (again playing himself) into producing a true ghost story video for them to star in. In 2016, Shiraishi also published a "fake documentary textbook" whose subtitle—"depicting the 'lie' of reality through movies" (*riaritī no aru 'uso' wo egaku eiga hyōgen*)—shows that he is clearly aware of his oeuvre's complicated relationship with the real.

Similar to the process of creating idol brands, images, and illusions of intimacy between idols and fans, found-footage horror films use the appearance of realness—actors who don't appear to be acting (and sometimes use their real names), unprofessional-looking camera work and editing, and careful manipulation of any and all media (web content, social media postings, and commercials) related to their film—to create a fictional spectacle. As with idol culture, a sort of cognitive dissonance is required on the part of the fans, who are aware that what they are watching is fiction, but derive pleasure from it by supporting the illusion of its realness. Found-footage horror films' combination of amateurish aesthetics and claims of authenticity "playfully collapses the boundaries separating the depicted universe from reality, and by extension challenges the ontological status of the film as a self-contained object" (Sayad 2016). The found-footage horror film is presented as "a fragment of the real world, and the implication is that this material might well spill over into it" (45). For the audience, fear and discomfort (which constitutes a kind of pleasure for the horror fan) come not only from the presence of ghosts or supernatural happenings but also from the sense that the boundaries between the real world and the film world are thin.

For fans of idols, the idols' appearances in horror films (as well as paratexts like TV interviews, promotional events, and pamphlets produced for the films) are one component in a "database" for fans to connect with. Today, found-footage horror films also benefit from a consumer culture in which a large percentage of media is consumed via private computers or phones, in the darkness of one's own room instead of in the crowded space of a public movie theater. Experiencing the film in an informal environment, as if it were simply a chance YouTube encounter or a link posted on social media, adds to the feeling of authenticity.[4] Even if the "cross-purposed interaction" of devices such as the TV screen, computer screen, and movie screen may mean that "the medium is no longer the message in the digital age" (Negroponte 1995, 71, quoted in Friedberg 2006, 4), in the case of found-footage horror, the frame through which one views the narrative—a computer screen, a smart phone screen, and a movie screen—has an impact on the experience. As we will see in the case of *Shirome*, the genre is also well suited to expose, intentionally or not, the tension between authenticity and illusion at the heart of idol culture.

PSYCHIC VISION AND *SHIROME*: GHOST POVS AND LAYERS OF REALITY/PERFORMANCE

Watching *Shirome* and its portrayal of both idol culture and supernatural dangers, it's hard not to think of *Psychic Vision*, the short, made-for-video horror film released a decade before *Ringu* and eight years before Nakata's *Don't Look Up* (which contains many plot elements and images similar to those found in *Ringu*). Like *Shirome*, *Psychic Vision* focuses on the world of pop idols, and like so much J-horror that came after, it "showcases terrors generated by media and technology" (Kinoshita 2009, 235 n.31). Kinoshita notes that the film "garnered cult followings from amateur and professional horror fans, including (Kiyoshi) Kurosawa and (Hiroshi) Takahashi" (235 n.31). As in *Shirome*, in *Psychic Vision* images of an eternally youthful, upbeat idol performer singing and posing for the camera are juxtaposed with ghostly happenings, as well as the idea that the song the idol is promoting might be cursed (due to the suicide of the songwriter several years before).[5] The film moves between a collection of footage meant to be broadcast as part of the promotional campaign for the idol's new song, some of which seems to have captured a ghost in the background, as well as other "found" videotape footage that reveals strange happenings throughout the campaign, and ultimately footage that seems to indicate that the idol and one of the producers have been attacked by some sort of malevolent spirit. Mysterious images of a woman in white or fainter images of what appears to be a woman holding a baby appear in the background of various video and photo shoots, with one character declaring them *shinrei shashin* (ghost photographs). Music recordings reveal ghostly sounds. Ghosts are seeping into the real world via photographic cameras, video cameras, audio systems, and video tapes, yet again forcing us to "become aware of the uncanny nature of the process of capturing an image itself" (Gunning 2013, 226). Beyond the presence of actual ghosts, characters in the film must deal with the inherent spectrality of the media devices and technologies that are essential for building an idol's brand.

In the film's final moments, we see what is described as a "re-edit" (*saihenshū*) of footage from idol Kato Emi's music video shoot—not only a mix of footage that the reporting team filmed but also "mysterious footage" (*fukaika na eizō*) that they did not record, including static and close-up images of people contorting in agony as they are seemingly attacked by spirits. In this "mysterious footage," the camera seems to fly around like a ghost. At one point, it hovers high above reporter Kyōko's head, and she addresses it directly. We then cut to on-screen text that reads simply, "Whose POV was this?" Indeed, was this the point of view of a camera? Or was it the point of view of a ghost?[6] Was the camera *itself* possessed by a ghost? In *Psychic Vision*, we are not only bombarded with images of ghosts but also made to see the world through ghostly eyes, and our "ghost POV" as spectators reminds us of the inherent spectrality of video and photography itself.

Shirome also presents itself as the making of a promotional TV segment, the kind that idols and idol groups frequently appear in. The film documents an idol group, Momoiro Clover Z, being exposed to frightening ghost stories, often shrieking in terror, and journeying to an abandoned school to ask the god Shirome to grant their wish. Momoiro Clover Z (formerly known as Momoiro Clover) are a fairly typical idol group, though their branding and origin story have strived to set them apart from the more well-known AKB48. Initially formed in 2008, the group has usually consisted of four to six female members between the ages of thirteen and nineteen. Like most idol groups, they present an image of youthfulness and innocence, speaking in high-pitched voices, wearing brightly colored costumes, not openly dating, and performing songs with cheerful lyrics and heavily choreographed dance moves. Their origin story emphasizes the kind of can-do spirit that many fans admire in idols—they initially began performing in parks on weekends while still students and gradually built up a fan base, eventually debuting a successful single in 2009 and performing on the popular year-end singing competition Kōhaku Uta-Gassen in 2012, 2013, and 2014.[7] Membership has shifted over time as performers have "graduated" or aged out of the group. *Shirome* stars six of the group members: Momota Kanako, Hayami Akari, Tamai Shiori, Sasaki Ayaka, Ariyasu Momoka, and Takagi Reni.

In *Shirome*, we are presented with a "record" of the making of a ghost hunting TV segment in which the members of Momoiro Clover Z are told that they need to enter an abandoned school, perform a song and dance, and ask an ancient god to grant their wish to perform on the annual Kōhaku singing competition show. Our sense of what is "real" is uncertain from the very beginning—the story of "Shirome" was invented for the film, but in an early scene, it is presented as if it is an established urban legend. In a lengthy interview with Inaho Radio, Shiraishi said that he made a point of mixing reality and fiction in the film. Realizing that Momoiro Clover Z member Hayami Akari was fairly skilled at acting, for example, Shiraishi decided to secretly tell her to say certain things and behave a certain way (pretending to be possessed by a spirit, for example). Momota Kanako was also told to describe a dream that she'd had. Otherwise, though, the members of Momoiro Clover Z were kept mostly in the dark about the nature of the film shoot, believing that they were filming a promotional TV segment (Inaho Radio 2019). Thus, the confusion and fear on their faces—as when Hayami Akari appears to be possessed by a demon—seems quite real, even if Momoiro Clover Z probably did not believe they were actually going to be killed by demons (and were surely familiar with Japanese TV's long history of setting people up to be pranked or frightened). Regardless of how much the girls may have been aware that the supernatural happenings around them were not "real," in the film, they are *presented* as if they are unaware that everything is staged, and they do a fairly convincing job of appearing as if they are not at all in on the joke.

The genuine terror that Momoiro Clover Z seem to be experiencing—evidenced in their high-pitched shrieks, frequent cries of "stop it" (*iya da*) or "I can't, I can't" (*muri, muri*)—is quite convincing. But within the world of pop idols, it is common to perform or exaggerate raw emotion—especially tears, which are on frequent display whenever the performers watch moving video footage on a TV show or speak heartfelt words at a "graduation" ceremony. (There were many tears when Momoiro Clover member Hayami

Akari announced publicly that she was leaving the group to pursue an acting career.) Such emotion isn't necessarily fake, but it is expressed with the knowledge that this is what the audience/fans want to see. Galbraith and Karlin note that tears are central to idol events, which are often structured to allow for moments of crying. Such tears are a form of "release, which idols facilitate"—crying and tears are "prohibited in so many other parts of life" (Galbraith and Karlin 2020, 63), and thus the moments when idols and fans cry together strengthen their sense of community and feel like a rejection of certain societal rules. Found-footage horror, and horror films more generally, also serve as a form of catharsis for many fans, with bodily tension usually followed by a sense of relief when the film is over.[8]

Real fear and discomfort also allow fans to further take on the role of "supporter" or protector, and thus while *Shirome* is clearly not a documentary, both the film and its marketing use the trappings of realness effectively. In TV interviews promoting the film the members of Momoiro Clover Z repeatedly talk about how they were "genuinely scared" and how their managers and other members of the production staff were "really good actors" who made them feel as if the supernatural events depicted in the film were real (tokoroda 2014; Movie Collection 2010). In one discussion on Yahoo! Japan, user leoleo_day asked for reassurance that Akari Hayami was "really acting" when she appeared to be possessed, and other commenters assured them that this was the case (Yahoo! Japan 2011). (Shiraishi also hinted in his interview with Inaho Radio that some fans were unhappy with him for making the movie, believing that he had treated Momoiro Clover Z badly [Inaho Radio 2019].) Momoiro Clover Z's terror and suffering in *Shirome* also serves a specific function in the idol world—a chance to see pop idols experiencing raw emotion and a chance for fans to feel that emotion with them. Those moments of raw emotion are yet another piece of a "database" for fans to engage with (as seen in discussions like the one on the Yahoo! Japan forum mentioned above).

Like *Psychic Vision*, *Shirome* plays with the notion of who is watching whom, and to what extent the images in a found-footage horror film can lead us to a sense of "truth." As in so many found-footage horror films, in *Shirome*, we begin with voiceover telling us that all the answers are within the video, reminding us that "revealing" is "the essence of technology" (Heidegger 1977 [1954], 12). But what we see in the film often serves more to reinforce the uncertainty about what is "real" and what is a performance. After the moment at the end of the film when Shiraishi and the staff reveal to Momoiro Clover Z that everything was a joke, the credits roll, but then the scene in which Hayami Akari appears to be possessed is played again. Shiraishi calls "cut" repeatedly, the other members of Momoiro Clover Z look confused and uncertain, and Hayami does not stop screaming. In his interview with Inaho Radio, Shiraishi indicated he wanted to keep the audience uncertain as to whether everything was meant to be a joke or not, and that mixing fiction and reality (*hontō no bubun to feiku no bubun*) made the film more interesting. Shiraishi also used nonactors in some roles: the older woman playing the spiritual medium, Sō Yūko, is in fact a medium who has made many TV appearances (Shiraishi describes her behavior in the film as "the real thing" [*honmono*] [Inaho Radio 2019]). In the same moment that the film "reveals" things to us, it also obscures, or at least hides certain truths.

In one scene near the beginning of *Shirome*, we see director Shiraishi (playing himself) talking to the members of Momoiro Clover Z around a table in a dressing room. The cameraperson and boom mic (of the person who is ostensibly filming everything for a TV segment) are clearly visible in some shots. After telling the girls what they will do the next day, he tells them each to look at the camera and talk about their feelings about the day's events and tomorrow's shoot, specifically using the word *honne* (true self / true feelings). One by one, they stand directly in front of the camera and make some version of the same speech: they are scared and uncertain, but in order to achieve their dream of appearing on Kōhaku, they will *ganbaru* (persist/do their best). Occasionally, the camera cuts away to someone else watching all of this on the screen of a portable DVD player. As the girls make their "confessions," they speak directly into the camera, and we can also see a mirror and another stationary camera behind them (figure 2.2). One of the girls, Sasaki Ayaka, sings her usual self-introduction song, rubbing her "squishy" (*puni puni*) and "squeaky clean" (*kyu kyu*) cheeks and encouraging all of the other girls to sing along.

Figure 2.2 The members of Momoiro Clover Z confess their "true feelings" to the camera in *Shirome* (Shiraishi Kōji 2010). *Source*: Screenshot taken by author.

In the background, Hayami Akari shows her discomfort with the situation by fidgeting and shifting in her chair. When it's her turn to speak, she expresses her opposition to the plan, saying that she won't be able to perform. The other girls fidget uncomfortably but ultimately tell her "It's okay, keep going"—and then the lights suddenly go out and we hear all of the girls scream.

Watching this scene, we get a sense of the multiple layers of reality and performance operating within the film. First, there is the found-footage horror convention of showing us the unpolished, amateurish version of what is on screen (the clearly visible man holding the boom mic and the director planning out the shoot for the next day). We see another familiar trope when the camera moves between close-ups of each individual girl's face (found-footage horror often includes segments in which people talk directly to the camera/audience). In these confessional moments, the girls are supposedly expressing their *honne*, their true feelings, but we also see that they are performing—making cute gestures for the camera, singing cutesy songs, and vowing to persevere (*ganbaru*) through everything. One girl is also playing up her discomfort with the whole situation by making sure that we see her fidgeting in the background. When the lights go out in the middle of this girl's "confession," and we hear a cacophony of screams, it feels like the "performance" has been interrupted and the girls are feeling real terror. Via the cuts to others watching everything on a DVD player screen and the presence of the mirror and stationary camera in the dressing room, we also get the sense that everything we, the viewer, are watching is also being watched (and evaluated) by someone else.

The confessions, the performative discomfort, the shrieks of terror, and the cutesy singalongs can also be seen as parts of the database—pieces of a narrative whole that idol fans can consume. In their perceived "roughness," these moments allow fans to feel a closer connection to the idols, or to feel like a "supporter." And the constant shifting of who is looking or being looked at forces viewers to repeatedly reevaluate their own perspective and position. This sense of looking/being looked at and the many different screens, frames, and points of reference that *Shirome* presents us with are also visible in a scene where the girls spend the night in their dance studio. The scene begins with Momota Kanako filming herself and the other girls with a miniature video camera, asking each girl for comments on their situation. The camera switches back and forth between Momota's "selfie" view and the view of a stationary camera placed within the room. Asked for her comment, Hayami Akari quietly says: "We're being watched from above" (*ue kara miraretieru*) (Shiraishi 2010b). After the girls go to sleep, the stationary camera records their sleeping bodies in the dark, along with strange balls of light that move across the screen. The footage is occasionally broken up with static. The next day, Hayami Akari says that she dreamed that she woke up and saw a large pair of eyes on the ceiling watching her.

Scenes like this reveal that idol groups like Momoiro Clover Z are indeed being watched all the time, if not by actual ghosts. Within the film, they film themselves and perform their "cutesy" idol personae for the camera. A stationary camera records them when they are not "on" (but the camera is not hidden, and surely, they behave differently in front of it). This stationary camera also turns us, the viewers, into voyeurs, allowing us to watch them while they sleep. The footage captured for this film is shown to us again in slow motion, or shown framed within a portable DVD player being viewed by the director or another member of the crew. Throughout the film, we "jump" between different camera and frame perspectives, some meant to be more "raw" and "real" than others but all of them infused with the elements of performance that are central to being an idol. Before the girls enter the abandoned school building, they show us their minicameras, telling us that they will record everything and convey it to us (*otsutae dekiru yō ni totte kimasu*) (Shiraishi 2010b). As they move through the school, we shift constantly between the "selfie" perspectives of their minicameras and the cameras of the professional film crew (with boom mics, lights, and camera equipment often visible in the frame). The minicamera footage shows the girls alternately terrified, cheerfully smiling, weeping, and singing to keep their spirits up, revealing the constant tension between their idol personae and the "reality" that is always just beneath the surface. When they finally perform their cheerful song and dance number for Shirome before asking the god to grant their wish, near the end the footage is broken up with static and the CD player malfunctions. The girls keep singing a capella and smiling, but it feels like a big part of the illusion has broken down.

In the same moment that *Shirome* mixes perspectives and frames, it also presents us with a variety of newer and older media devices and methods of dissemination, often positioned close to one another within scenes or within the narrative of the film. These images remind us of the changes in how horror stories are told, or the way that they are often presented via a variety of platforms and storytelling styles. Characters in *Shirome* film themselves on miniature video cameras (soon to be replaced by the ubiquitous presence of smart phone cameras). We watch Momoiro Clover Z watching someone else on a portable DVD player, another media device that would soon become obsolete in the wake of streaming and the practice of playing DVDs on a computer.

And then there are the much older methods of telling stories, illustrated via the *kaidanshi*, or ghost storyteller, who relays his stories verbally. In one scene, multiple media devices and modes of dissemination are physically placed next to each other. The *kaidanshi* stands and tells his story orally, punctuating it with sound effects that he produces with his voice. He then shows the girls video footage of a man telling a story of a ghostly encounter, which they watch on a portable DVD player that is positioned next to a singing bowl and a candle. We watch the girls watching the DVD footage on the device, with the camera's perspective shifting between an image of the girls watching the DVD player next to the bowl and the candle, the DVD footage itself, and occasional shots of boom mics and crewmembers in the background. Eventually, the camera again focuses on the *kaidanshi*, who resumes telling the story orally. The singing bowl, the portable DVD player, the professional cameras and microphones, the oral storyteller, and finally our own perspective as spectators, watching all of this through the screen of a phone, a tablet, a computer, or a television—layers upon layers of mediation that remind us of the ways that those devices serve to further "fracture" our sense of what is real with a found-footage horror film's narrative.

In its juxtaposition of many different media devices, screens, and frames-within-frames, *Shirome* reveals the changing ways that horror stories are told, consumed, and shared. Like the urban legends of 2channel, which have been disseminated via word of mouth, newspapers, online forums, and film, *Shirome* juxtaposes an in-person *kaidan* storytelling event with a DVD interview, both elements embedded within the *Shirome* film itself. The girls watch the *kaidanshi* and the video interview, and we watch both of them via the film—perhaps viewed in a movie theater, but more likely at home via a DVD or online streaming service. Like the many layers of frames and perspectives present in *Shirome* and other films like it, the ghost story itself is now heavily mediated, presented in multiple forms (sometimes all at once) via a film that can be consumed in a variety of ways.

CONCLUSION

In *Shirome*, the worlds of idols and found-footage horror come together to reveal the ways that both worlds are founded on "mutual agreement" and performative authenticity. A professional film made to look amateur presents us with a group of young women whose success hinges on their "unpolished" personae—personae that are every bit as carefully crafted as the amateur and accidental look of the film. We are not seeing reality, but a spectacle of the real: a performance of authenticity that is augmented by the presence of many different filmed perspectives, images of cameras and microphones that would normally be edited out, and performative cheerfulness and terror on the part of the idols. Like so much found-footage horror, it presents itself as an unedited record of facts that will reveal all, but just as much is obscured as revealed.

Shirome, then, is indeed a "record" of many things. It presents itself as footage from a promotional TV segment that will provide us with "answers" to a certain mystery. It is a record of seemingly authentic terror experienced by young women who to a certain extent are defined by their willingness to suffer and persevere (*gaman*) for the benefit of their fans—fans who may consume images of their suffering as components of a "database." It is a record of stories recorded and conveyed through many different media devices that further fracture any sense of certainty about what is real/fake within the narrative. It is a collection of frames and screens, often juxtaposed next to or layered on top of one another. In the end, what gets left out of the frame—what remains beyond the reach of the viewer, though still connected to the larger whole—is a sense of absolute "truth." *Shirome* exists in the "forest of narrativities" (de Certeau 1984 [1980], 186) through which our everyday lives are now defined. It is a small narrative that serves as a piece of a grand narrative (or grand nonnarrative), in much the same way as widely circulated images of idols serve as pieces of a whole for fans to collect and engage with, giving them access to a "relationship" with idols and the larger idol universe.

NOTES

1. My thanks to a student in Colleen Laird's undergraduate class at the University of British Columbia, who described K-pop stars as polished professionals and Japanese idols as "always a work in progress."

2. Though the privileging of looks and personality over talent in pop music stars is hardly unique to Japan, a lack of even the most basic singing and dancing abilities is arguably more noticeable among Japanese idols. Their dance moves are closer to gestures (easily imitated by fans), and their singing often sounds closer to speech or shouting.

3. *Tarento*, or "talent," are Japanese media personalities who appear in commercials, live TV programs, movies, and fictional TV shows. Some may also be singers or release the occasional single. They are typically young and conventionally attractive and are generally celebrated for their "everyday" personalities and appearance. For more on *tarento*, see Gabriella Lukacs' *Scripted Affects, Branded Selves: Television, Subjectivity, and Capitalism in 1990s Japan* (2010).

4. My thanks to a peer reviewer of a different version of this chapter who pointed out that their students find found-footage films more convincing if they are watching them at home instead of at a movie theater. I would argue that certain films like the horror film *Unfriended* (dir. Levan Gabriadze 2014), which takes place entirely within the confines of a Skype video conversation, are definitely taking advantage of this tendency. Miranda Larsen has described horror movies that take place within the confines of a computer screen as "desktop horror" or "screen life horror" (2019). This kind of movie is more unsettling when watched on an actual computer, where the viewer's personal screen icons and incidental computer noises may mirror what is happening within the film.

5. Voiceover at the very beginning of *Shirome* mentions a "rumor" that Momoiro Clover Z is cursed. The idea of cursed idols or idol songs (and the potential of idol songs to "brainwash" listeners) also appears in the films *Contagious Song* (*Densen uta*, 2007, dir. Harada Masato), starring members of AKB48, and *Suicide Club* (*Jisatsu sākuru*, 2001, dir. Sono Sion).

6. Pinedo (1997, 52) describes this kind of camera work as "unclaimed point of view shot" (Scherer 2016, 75 n.14).

7. As with most idol groups, the exact nature of the group's formation is difficult to ascertain. The "origin story" that I describe here is the one that is repeated in the *Shirome* film and on various Japanese- and English-language websites (Momoiro Clover Z Wiki 2014; Momoiro Clover Z Live History 2018).

8. For more on "body genres" (films that produce a physical response), see Linda Williams' 1991 essay "Film Bodies: Gender, Genre, and Excess."

Chapter 3

The Haunted Forest
Circulating Aokigahara

Ōsawa Shinichi's music video for his instrumental electronic piece "Paris" begins with dark, slightly blurred images of dense tree growth and moss-covered boulders that almost resemble an alien landscape. As the music plays, a shower of broken crystals moves across the frame, blurring and creating multiple, tiny images of the forest. Eventually, these crystals merge into the image of a young woman who dances in slow motion within the forest as a spotlight flashes. Throughout the video, images of the forest and the woman coalesce and break apart—just when we think we have a clear sense of what the space looks like, the image shatters and re-forms again. It is not necessarily frightening, but the imagery is eerie—everything in the video feels ephemeral and constantly shifting, a representation of a spectral, otherworldly space (Ōsawa 2010).

Ōsawa's music video was filmed in Aokigahara, the forest at the base of Mt. Fuji that is known as a place where many have died by suicide. Out of hundreds of visual representations of Aokigahara, from music videos to comedy sketches to prefecture-approved hiking courses, Ōsawa's video perhaps most succinctly illustrates the way that images of the forest have been captured, reshaped, and disseminated across Japan and the world. Like the fragmented and re-forming images in this video, the narrative that has emerged of Aokigahara as alternately haunted, sad, dangerous, and exotic is a fractured one, blurry and clear, existing in pieces culled from blog posts, films, Japanese tourism pamphlets, novels, and YouTube videos. The circulation of images and narratives of Aokigahara also reveals a great deal about the changing nature of how scary stories, and in particular scary stories about Japan, are told, and the role that "authenticity" plays in constructing certain horror narratives. Representations of Aokigahara rely on a mix of truth and myth, with certain details privileged over others to create a kind of fictionalized spectacle.

What role does "authenticity" play in the creation of Aokigahara-focused films and YouTube videos? How do Japanese and non-Japanese perceptions of Aokigahara fit into the framework of Orientalist representations of Japan? Finally, what role does new media play in films about Aokigahara, in the circulation and shaping of perceptions of Aokigahara, and in the depiction of Aokigahara as a "ghostly" or "haunted" space? In beginning to answer these questions, I will first examine the way that images and stories of Aokigahara have been circulated in Japanese-speaking networks via YouTube, television, and films, focusing on the 2021 film *Suicide Forest Village* (*Jukai mura*, dir. Takashi Shimizu). I will then examine the forest's depiction in English-speaking networks via YouTube, online journalism, and films, focusing on the film *The Forest* (dir. Jason Zada 2016). In examining the many ways that Aokigahara is "framed" via different forms of media and media devices, I will also illustrate how these different frames and screens force the viewer to constantly shift their perspective, producing a sense of "fractured reality" that also reveals the spectrality not only of the forest but also of different forms of media and media devices.

AOKIGAHARA: HISTORY AND REPRESENTATION IN JAPAN

Aokigahara sits at the base of Mt. Fuji and covers approximately 35 square kilometers. It is commonly referred to as the Aokigahara *jukai*, or "sea of trees," due to the fact that the large stretch of uniform, unbroken forest resembles an ocean when viewed from above. It was formed after an eruption of Mt. Fuji in the ninth century, which covered the area with volcanic rock. Trees and moss eventually consumed the rocky, uneven ground, creating a dense, uniform forest that can be hazardous to walk through outside of its human-made paths (the volcanic rock of the forest floor is covered in slippery moss and is full of fissures). The denseness of the tree growth means that the forest is remarkably quiet and also easy to get lost in—off the paths everything looks the same in every direction, and in certain parts of the forest, compasses are reported to malfunction.[1]

Information is mixed on when and how, exactly, Aokigahara became associated with suicide. Endō writes that Mt. Fuji's religious significance within Buddhism, as well as the fact that the mountain and the area around it were barren, rocky, and uninhabitable, made them ideal places to carry out the final stages of *nyūjō*, a lengthy process of religious self-mummification. One of the first recorded examples of such a *nyūjō* in Aokigahara was the 1340 death of a monk named Shōkai (Endō 1967, 198). More generally, Aokigahara's proximity to the sacred space of Mt. Fuji made it a popular site for ritual suicide by monks (Rich 2018; Suzuki 2019). Takahashi writes that before World War II, many people believed that "once a person had entered the forest, it would be impossible to find a way out, and subsequently many people tried to take their own lives in Jukai" (Takahashi 1988, 165–166). The prefecture no longer reveals the number of bodies found every year in the forest, though it is believed that numbers have declined to around 30 per year since the early 2000s, when as many as 100 bodies might be found in a single year (Rich 2018). According to police reports, fifty-four bodies were recovered in 2010 (Gilhooly 2011). The actual number may be higher, as the forest's large size makes finding every body difficult.

Though the number of bodies tends to rise and fall with Japan's overall suicide rate (which has tended to rise and fall with unemployment rates [Motohashi 2011, 1282]), recent efforts by the prefecture and by private individuals—training volunteers to stop and talk to people who seem to be going into the forest to die, installing cameras at the entrances, and posting signs with phone numbers for a mental health hotline—maybe helping to reduce the number of suicides. In 2017, the "Connect Life Network" (*Inochi wo tsunagu nettwāku*) published a detailed suicide prevention guide on the Yamanashi Prefecture website, which included advice on how to approach someone in the forest who might be there to take their own life (Yamanashi Prefecture 2019). As of January 2021, though, the suicide rate in Yamanashi Prefecture remained significantly higher than rates in other prefectures (*Mainichi Shinbun* 2021). Suffice it to say that while the numbers may not be as dramatic as many blog posts and videos indicate, the number of suicides in and around Aokigahara continues to be significant.

Aokigahara has been depicted (albeit briefly) in a variety of Japanese TV programs, comic books, films, and anime series. The forest appears in the manga version of the zombie story *I Am a Hero*. There are references to the forest in the anime series *Mazinger Z* (*Majingā zetto* 1972–1974), *Tokyo Ghoul* (*Tōkyō gūru* 2014–2018), *Transformers: Super-God Masterforce* (*Toransufōmā: Chōjin masutāfōsu* 1988–1989), and *Samurai Deeper Kyo* (*Samurai dīpā kyō* 2002), the manga *The Kurosagi Corpse Delivery Service* (*Kurosagi shitai takuhaibin* 2002–), and in the video games *Inazuma Eleven 2* (*Inazuma irebun 2: Kyōi no shinryakusha* 2009), and *Tokyo Dark* (*Tokyo dāku* 2017). The forest has also been the subject of several TV programs, where it is frequently presented as a scenic hiking spot, as in a 2014 episode of the Fuji TV series *Nonfix* called "Walking the Aokigahara Sea of Trees" (*Aokigahara jukai wo aruku* 2014), and a 2016 episode of the popular NHK series *Buratamori*, in which TV personality Tamori explored the forest (*Buratamori* 2016). "Demystifying" Aokigahara and presenting it as a pleasant place for sightseeing is very much in line with Yamanashi Prefecture's "re-branding"[2]

On YouTube, Japanese depictions of Aokigahara are somewhat less sensitive. Though the infamous Logan Paul video[3] that seemed to make light of suicide in Aokigahara received plenty of criticism both inside and outside Japan, Japanese YouTube videos that focus on Aokigahara are also a mix of typical comedy/prank videos and documentary-style pieces. One, from the YouTube channel Hekitora Hausu, features a group of men in Christmas-themed costumes stumbling upon a corpse in Aokigahara—which is then revealed to be one of their friends (Hekitora Hausu 2017). Some videos have a "true ghost story" feel, like a video of a group of comedians playing *kokkuri-san* (a Ouija-like game in which participants move a coin between letters and numbers to communicate with spirits) in a tent in Aokigahara (Broiler Chicken and Yoshie Mori 2011). Some are crude, like a video entitled "Extreme Nipple Sumo in Aokigahara," which features men in Aokigahara at night pulling clothespins off their lips and nipples and screaming in pain (Makuch Leonie 2014). Another video from the popular YouTube channel Fischer's features two men playing Pokemon Go in Aokigahara (and falling down a great deal as they trip over tree roots) (Fischer's 2016).[4] On Japanese YouTube, at least, Aokigahara is hardly a taboo subject and is even sometimes presented in a (darkly) humorous way.

Matsumoto Seichō's 1960 novel *Tower of Waves* (*Nami no tō*), a tragic love story that ends with a woman dying by suicide in Aokigahara, is sometimes mentioned as a cause of increases in suicides in Aokigahara (*Studio 360* 2009), though there is no real evidence that the book's publication, or the release of any of its many film and TV adaptations, actually caused an increase in suicides. In the 1960 film version of *Tower of Waves* (dir. Nakamura Noboru), Aokigahara is above all presented as sad and serene. In the film's final scene, the protagonist Yoriko sits at a table overlooking a lake, the "sea of trees" spread out beneath her, Mt. Fuji in the background. We see that she is writing a letter to the lover she has decided she cannot be with, a glass bottle of pills in her hand. In the final shot of the film, we see her walking slowly into the dense growth of trees as orchestral music swells (Nakamura 1960). The vision of death and tragedy connected to Aokigahara in this version of *Tower of Waves* is decidedly romantic: a woman dies rather than live unhappily, and she does it by disappearing inside a primeval forest. There is no gore, no aftermath—we simply see her walk slowly into the forest as the music swells. Likewise, in a 1991 TV drama version of Matsumoto's novel, the final scene in Aokigahara is full of fog, and the actress playing Yoriko seems to actually disappear into the fog, like a ghost (Fujita 1991). The space of Aokigahara is mostly absent in the *Tower of Waves* novel and films, but its presence—and the romantic idea of selfless suicide in the name of love—loom large over the story.

A similarly romantic image of Aokigahara can be found in the film *Aokigahara* (dir. Shinjō Taku 2012), based on a short story of the same name by novelist (and former Tokyo governor) Ishihara Shintaro. In this story, a man living near the forest begins seeing ghostly images of another man in a yellow raincoat. It turns out that this ghost died by suicide with his lover in one of Aokigahara's famous caves, this time because she was dying of cancer and they could not be together (Shinjō 2012). Famously, it was this film's production that finally pushed Yamanashi Prefecture to explicitly forbid the shooting of films inside the forest without official permission—while early footage for the *Aokigahara* was shot in the forest, the shoot was eventually moved to a different forest in Shizuoka Prefecture (*Nihon Keizai Shinbun* 2012).

In both *Aokigahara* and *Tower of Waves*, Aokigahara embodies a kind of "undiscovered" aspect of Japan, a secret and mysterious place that is not only very much of Japan but also "exotic." It is a dark space, not in the sense that it is evil but in the sense that it is hidden and cut off from the rest of the world, the perfect place for a person like Yoriko and the doomed couple of *Aokigahara* to vanish. In the case of Yoriko, most likely there will be no body found, no remnant—Yoriko can truly disappear from the world, as so many who enter Aokigahara seem to want to do. These films are a mix of reality and self-Orientalizing fantasy—a real space, but one imbued with a long history of death and the romantic connections between suicide, tragic love stories, and places of scenic beauty, "oscillat[ing] between visibility and invisibility, presence and absence, materiality and immateriality" (Gunning 2013, 212). A haunted, spectral space made more so when presented via the "ghostly" medium of film and video. As we will see, other representations of Aokigahara in film imagine it as a different sort of "dark space," as well as mixing its "realness" with Orientalist fantasies of a strange and inscrutable Japan.

SUICIDE FOREST VILLAGE: FLYING OUT OF THE FRAME

Suicide Forest Village, directed by veteran J-horror director Shimizu Takashi, is the first Japanese film produced by a major studio (Tōei) to depict the forest in a supernatural/horrific context. It is the second in Shimizu's planned "scary village" (*kyōfu no mura*) trilogy, the first being *Howling Village* (*Inunaki mura*, dir. Shimizu Takashi 2019), which was partly inspired by the urban legend connected to the remote Inunaki region of Japan, where a brutal murder took place and a village is rumored to exist that is cut off from the rules and laws of Japan.[5] Like many films and videos that depict the forest,

Suicide Forest Village is built on a foundation of widely circulated images and narratives surrounding the real space of Aokigahara, but includes fantastical elements involving a secret village, a cursed box, and stories of *obasute* (literally "throwing away old people," the act of leaving one's elderly relatives in the forest or on top of a mountain to die, a practice that is believed by some [without much evidence] to have been widespread in Japan long ago). Interestingly, these fantastical elements may have been what convinced Yamanashi Prefecture to allow the film crew to shoot within Aokigahara— one of the official reasons given for lifting the ban on filming was the fact that the film did not explicitly depict suicide in Aokigahara, instead depicting a world fairly divorced from the forest's reality (*Sankei News* 2020).

Suicide Forest Village tells the story of two sisters, Mei and Hibiki, being raised by their grandmother after the death of their mother (possibly by suicide in Aokigahara). The younger Hibiki is withdrawn and sullen, finding comfort in an online group of occult enthusiasts. As Hibiki is watching a woman broadcast live from Aokigahara (the same YouTuber character and actress who appeared in *Howling Village*), the video abruptly cuts out. Soon after, Hibiki discovers a mysterious box that is later revealed to be a *kotoribako*, or "cursed box," which brings death to all who come near it. (The name *kotoribako* [child-taking box] points to the box's particular affinity for cursing children and pregnant women, though in *Suicide Forest Village* its curse seems to simply affect anyone who comes near it or touches it.) As the story unfolds, we learn that there are connections between the box, the mother's death, Aokigahara, and Hibiki's ability to sense the supernatural. It is revealed that many "undesirables" who had historically been abandoned in the forest have been living in a secret village within Aokigahara and have essentially fused with the forest, drawing others in and absorbing them into the flora.

Like so many other videos and films connected to Aokigahara, *Suicide Forest Village* mixes fact, supernatural fantasy, urban legends, and "invented" urban legends (something we have also seen in *Toshimaen: The Movie* and *Shirome*). Stories of Aokigahara as a place for *obasute* have circulated for a long time, as have stories of *kotoribako* (which apparently originated in the Japanese 2channel "Occult" group in 2005 [Kaidan News-c]). The film takes these fragments and weaves them together to imagine a secret "village" of ghosts who have possessed/been possessed by the forest. In the film's climactic scene, Mei has gone into the forest to try to discover what happened to her mother. Throughout the film, we have learned that Hibiki, like her mother, has always felt a connection to the strange and supernatural, and has felt that something within the forest was "calling" her. By the end of the film, Hibiki is in a mental institution, but the forest's energy is attacking her, appearing as shadows of creeping vines on the white walls of her hospital room that fling her body back and forth. At the same time, Hibiki's spirit is somehow present within the forest, where both sisters learn that their mother did not die by suicide—she entered the forest with her daughters to try to break the *kotoribako* curse and ultimately stayed behind so that they could escape. This time, as Mei flees, Hibiki's spirit sacrifices herself to save Mei and is absorbed by the forest and its villagers, a mix of hands, tree vines, and moss slowly enveloping her until she has become one with the village and the forest. For those watching in a theater, the scene has the potential to be enhanced by the use of MX4D, technology that "augments" the viewing experience with tactile sensations, movement of the theater seats, smells, and sounds. Throughout the film, the boundaries between the audience and the screen are frequently broken by blasts of cold air, shifting seats that simulate walking, or the feeling of objects brushing against feet. We are literally put in the place of certain characters on the screen. As the vines creep over Hibiki's body, a thin hose under the theater seat tickles the viewer's legs, imitating the feeling of the vines. Wind through the trees manifests as actual cold air on our faces. The distinction between reality and fiction, actual Internet rumor and invented urban legend is further blurred by the presence of technology designed to make the experience of watching the film more "real."

Suicide Forest Village also provides an example of the important role that new media plays both within the narrative and in the marketing of Japanese horror films, and the role that certain in-theater technologies play in making a film experience even more intimate and realistic. Early in the film, we see a YouTuber, "Akkīna," broadcasting live from Aokigahara as comments appear on the screen (similar scenes open both *Toshimaen: The Movie* and *Sadako 3D*, discussed in chapters 1 and 4). Such a scene is familiar from YouTube, where many Japanese and non-Japanese creators have filmed themselves walking through Aokigahara (like Akkīna, often with selfie sticks, underscoring the fact that the video is not so much about Aokigahara as it is about *them in* Aokigahara). Akkīna is bright and cheerful, describing her surroundings and marking her path through the forest with red tape. For those watching the film in a theater, as Akkīna walks over the uneven ground of the forest, the MX4D technology causes the theater seats to rock and vibrate slightly—we feel as if we are walking with her, not just watching from our seats. At one point, she sees a man in the distance and follows him, but he seems to vanish. She becomes frightened, showing viewers that her compass and GPS are not working, details that are a frequent feature of Aokigahara-focused YouTube videos (figure 3.1). She follows her red tape back to her starting point but then sees that it is connected to a corpse hanging from a tree. Akkīna falls to the ground and the video grows staticky, cutting in and out before revealing a final shot of Akkīna's unconscious body and a pair of

Figure 3.1 The "Akkīna" character in the film *Suicide Forest Village* (Shimizu Takashi 2021). *Source*: Screenshot taken by author.

moss-covered legs moving into the frame. The camera then cuts to Hibiki's black computer screen—she has been watching the video alone in her room.

As with *Howling Village, Toshimaen: The Movie*, and the later *Ringu* sequels, our gateway to the frightening space of Aokigahara in *Suicide Forest Village* is a new media object: an amateur video broadcast over the Internet and viewed on a computer screen. This video-within-the-film is steeped in familiar information about Aokigahara that many viewers may have encountered online: the idea that compasses and GPS devices don't work, the image of a cheerful young person walking through the forest and commenting on how creepy it is, and the way that the broadcaster fosters intimacy by directly addressing the viewers/commenters. It is also ephemeral, appearing one moment on Hibiki's computer screen (and within the frame through which we, the spectators, are watching the *Suicide Forest Village* film) and then vanishing, reminding us of the ways that the specter "is both visible and invisible . . . a trace that marks the present with its absence in advance" (Derrida and Stiegler 2013, 38). The video, like the space it depicts, is imbued with a ghostly presence. It also plays with our sense of perspective—if we watch the film and the video-within-the-film on a computer, as many now do, we might momentarily forget that we are watching a film and imagine that we are yet again seeing Aokigahara through the frame/window of an online video. Watching it in a theater, though, brings an added layer of "reality"—the sensation of movement, sudden gusts of air, and even soft objects tickling our ankles as tree vines or hands reach for the characters on the screen, effectively embedding us in the experience with them, and then the MX4D technology stops and we are faced with Hibiki's black computer screen, reminding us that we are watching a video-within-a-film. As with so many depictions of new media and new media objects in Japanese horror films, we are repeatedly forced to shift perspective and literally/figuratively reframe our perceptions.

The "Akkīna" video-within-the-film also breaks diegetic borders in another way. As part of a "collaboration" with Yamanashi Prefecture, the *Suicide Forest Village* team filmed a short video segment of actress Ōtani Rinka as Akkīna marveling at the natural beauty of Aokigahara, with text and voiceover describing it as a "power spot" (a place believed to be full of healing energy), a "mysterious primeval forest," and a "place in Japan that one must go to" (Movie Collection 2021) (figure 3.2). The character of Akkīna, still played by Ōtani Rinka, also has her own actual YouTube channel, *Akkīna TV* (the name of the channel that appeared in the *Suicide Forest Village* film). It has been active since July 31, 2020, and contains videos of the actress as "Akkīna" eating spicy ramen, cooking, and exercising (*Akkīna TV* 2021).

One article describing the way that Akkīna/Ōtani moved between the "scary village" films and YouTube actually described her as "flying out of the screen and into the real world" (*sukurīn o tobidete genjitsu no sekai ni tōjō* [Nifty News 2020]). The character in the film exists in multiple contexts and within several different frames and screens, easily "flying" from one to the other. Though the *Akkīna TV* channel has few followers, the collaboration video was tweeted many times in the lead-up to the film's release on February 5, 2021, and as of March 2021, it had over 340,000 views on YouTube. These paratexts are both inside and outside the film's narrative, outside of the screen and inside it, part of what Alexander Galloway might call a "diegetic circuit" that forces us to think of the image as "a process, rather than as a set of discrete, immutable items" (Galloway 2013, 627). In its representation of

Figure 3.2 The "Akkīna" character in a video promoting the scenic beauty of Aokigahara. *Source*: Screenshot taken by author.

Aokigahara, *Suicide Forest Village*'s shift between the diegetic and nondiegetic world reinforces the connection between the two.

Suicide Forest Village is also one of the first feature films since 2012 to not only be given official permission to shoot in the forest but also to be part of an official collaboration with the prefectural government. Reports indicate that after initially rejecting the film crew's application to film in Aokigahara, the governor of Yamanashi Prefecture, Nagasaki Kōtarō, met with Toei executives and decided to "embrace" the scary image of the forest as a way to promote suicide prevention (*Sankei News* 2020). Officially, at least, part of the reason for this decision seems to be that, unlike the film *Aokigahara* or *Tower of Waves*, *Suicide Forest Village* does not romanticize suicide. In a sense, then, the film is "safe" because it depicts a fantastical version of Aokigahara, one that is frightening but does not focus on suicide specifically (*Sankei News* 2020). Viewers may be attracted to Aokigahara-focused videos, articles, and films because of their seeming authenticity, but for Yamanashi Prefecture the *lack* of authenticity was what made the film palatable.

With *Suicide Forest Village*, then, we see the way that new media objects both within the narrative of the film and in paratextual form (as promotional/PSA videos) serve to both fracture the reality/authenticity of Aokigahara and force a shift in perspective. Watching "Akkīna" in the video-within-the-film, we are reminded of actual YouTube and Niconico videos about Aokigahara, and might even forget that we are watching a film, since everything is "framed" within a YouTube-like window. But watching in a theater with MX4D technology, we are taken out of this frame when the seat rattles and moves in time with "Akkīna," literally putting us in her place. Then, watching the promotional video, we see Akkīna literally and figuratively "fly out of the screen," moving from her role as a frightened character in a horror film to a cheerful ambassador for the "power spot" version of Aokigahara, forcing us to reframe not only our position in relation to the video but also our imagining of Aokigahara itself.

Aokigahara and Japan as Other: Orientalism and "Distant Intimacy"

Representations of Aokigahara in English-language blog posts, news articles, YouTube videos, and films tend to follow an Orientalist narrative: presenting Japan and its people as alternately exotic, frightening, inscrutable, and alien. Edward Said's initial 1978 writings on Orientalism were primarily concerned with European perceptions of the Middle East (and the way those perceptions, which set the "Orient" up in opposition to the "Occident," helped Europe to further define *itself*). Today, though, phrases like "Orientalism" or "techno-Orientalism" (Morley and Robins 1995) are just as likely to refer to English-language representations of Japan, China, or Korea, and though historically the power relationship between, for example, the United States and Japan has been decidedly different from the power relationship between France and Vietnam, Richard Minear notes that

> By the time Europe and America began to deal with Japan . . . a set of attitudes formed during the exercise of political and military domination elsewhere had become a relatively inflexible state of mind. Hence we find Orientalist attitudes even in the absence of domination (Minear 1980, 516).

Japan may never have been *colonized* by the United States or Europe, but simply by virtue of not being part of Europe or the United States, it can still be imagined within an Orientalist framework—the power relationship is different, but the "set of attitudes" is already established.

Orientalism, Said argues, is not simply a set of falsehoods or fantasies—it is "a created body of theory and practice in which, for many generations, there has been a considerable material investment . . . an accepted grid for filtering through the Orient into Western consciousness" (Said 1978, 6). In the case of Japan and the work of anthropologists, travel writers, historians, and novelists, Orientalism means imagining Japan as mysterious and inscrutable where Europe and the United States are "normal" and knowable, imagining Japan as feminine where Europe and the United States are masculine, and imagining Japan as sexually free (or perverse) where Europe and the United States are conservative. Japan exists always in opposition to the "we" of whoever is depicting it, "expected to offer an endless series of strange and different things whereby the familiarity of *our* things (is) implicitly affirmed" (Sakai 1989, 116). In the case of Aokigahara, this often means framing the forest as dark, frightening, and "other" not only because of its connection to suicide but also because of its connection to Japan (and Japan's "strange" attitudes toward death and suicide).

Japan also has a history of "self-Orientalizing," both in the form of capitalizing on outsiders' perceptions of it and inventing or embellishing certain customs or national traits. Marilyn Ivy writes of how both the Discover Japan and Exotic Japan railway campaigns of the 1970s and 1980s attempted to re-define "Japanese-ness" and national-cultural identity. Discover Japan presented images of women traveling through rustic, traditional locations, while Exotic Japan was more of a pastiche, "incorporating both high-tech futurism and stereotypical Japanese high culture as signifiers of the exotic" (Ivy 1995, 48). Ofra Goldstein-Gidoni notes that Japanese conceptions of "traditional" culture are usually based in the idea of a fixed, unchanging Japanese past, and that the Japanese have always played an active role in "mythologizing" Japan and its history in much the same way that the non-Japanese have

(Goldstein-Gidoni 2001). Orientalism is not always a story of outsiders projecting their "exotic" image of a country onto that country; sometimes the exoticism is invented domestically, or sometimes foreign images of a country are embraced and capitalized on by the country itself.

English-language encounters with Japan, particularly those experienced through novels or films, are often experienced as travel to an exotic place with the comforting knowledge that (a) one is not actually traveling and (b) one will experience Japan, but not be overwhelmed by its otherness. In her analysis of readers' reactions to the popular novel *Memoirs of a Geisha* (Arthur Golden 1997), a fictional account of geisha life written by a North American male author, Anne Allison argues that there is a pattern of what she calls "distant intimacy: becoming intimate with the story, the world, and the characters . . . through the mediation of a distance that is orientalist (geisha and their world remain other in the end)" (Allison 2001, 384–385). This kind of "exotic escapism" is "akin to what bell hooks . . . means by 'getting a bit of the other: a thrilling escape that leaves both self and other intact after the ride'" (392–393). In other words, through reading a novel like this, one can get close to an alien world and group of people, even come to know them intimately, but at the end of the journey they are still other, and the visitor has not been completely absorbed into or seduced by their alien world.

Allison also notes that authenticity, or at least the aura of authenticity, is key to this kind of representation. Readers of *Memoirs of a Geisha* particularly liked the fact that the book was written by an expert on Japan—its "authentic aura" gave readers what Malek Alloula calls an "ethnographic alibi," which "allows women to fantasize Sayuri and geisha. Without this cover of being 'out there,' women would have to acknowledge the fantasies inspired by *Memoirs* as being theirs" (Allison 2001, 397). Reading an entirely made-up story about a mysterious world full of both sensuality and horrific sexual abuse and then imagining oneself *in* such a world, might be considered crude or disturbing, but because Golden's book is ostensibly based on historical fact, readers can assure themselves that they are simply engaging with a historical reality, not crafting "perverse" fantasies of their own. By extension, consuming (and even taking delight in) made-up stories of suicides in a remote forest might seem insensitive, but because Aokigahara is a real space, those who consume pictures, stories, and videos about Aokigahara can assure themselves that they are engaging with a historical and cultural reality. When a space like Aokigahara is experienced directly, it is usually a brief stop on a journey, not the final destination, allowing this sort of exotic space to remain "other" to those who visit it, even if the tourists in question have got a taste of something different. In these stories, the protagonists forge their deepest connections with other expatriates, while "the natives mostly have clearly assigned roles. Language teacher. Hangover healer. Dispenser of fortune cookie-style wisdom" (Roy 2010). These kinds of encounters with the other have barriers firmly in place, and distant intimacy allows the traveler to feel a sense of connection but never be completely consumed by an "alien" world.

In widely circulated digital media objects, Aokigahara frequently embodies this "distant intimacy": it is framed as exotic and strange both for its connection to death and because of its location in Japan. It is frequently described as "creepy" or "eerie." Sample online article titles include "15 Eerie Things about Japan's Suicide Forest" (Puchko 2016); "Japan's Suicide Forest Is Even Scarier Than It Sounds" (PopSugar Entertainment 2016); and "The 6 Creepiest Places on Earth" (Strusiewicz 2009). Creators often mention the fact that Japan has a high suicide rate and also claim that suicide is not taboo in Japan—claims that are not completely baseless but that neglect to explore the role that both *nihonjinron*[6] and Orientalist thinking play in the image of suicide in Japan.[7] In both amateur and professional journalism, certain falsehoods are repeated and unquestioned: the idea that *obasute* (the practice of leaving elderly people alone in the forest or on a mountain to die) was a documented and widespread practice (Keefe 2017, Nems 2015, Vice 2012), the idea that compasses do not work in the forest (Puchko 2016, Rear 2018), that it is always dark inside, that there are no animals and birds in Aokigahara, and that it is empty of people. The most common variety of YouTube video features people walking through the forest, sometimes at night, and commenting on its eeriness. The shaky camera work and minimal sound editing recall the found-footage horror aesthetic. Part of the appeal of these kinds of videos is clearly the thought of seeing a "real" place associated with death, but again, the commentary embellishes the experience to the point that what we see is a far cry from an "authentic" representation of Aokigahara.

A typical video, "Suicide Forest in Japan: Aokigahara, also known as the Sea of Trees," which had 294,000 views as of March 2021, begins with text that reads, "Graphic content viewer discretion is advised" in bright red (Tokyo DailyPhoto 2012). The video follows a group of Australian, United States, and Canadian tourists (all men) as they journey to Aokigahara for a camping trip. They make scary faces at the camera and joke about how many bodies they will see. About a third of the way into the video, slightly ominous music begins playing in the background. As they find pieces of tape tied to trees (often left behind by people who go into the forest to die) and an abandoned fire pit, the ominous music gets much louder. Two-thirds of the way through the video, they discover a corpse covered in maggots. The men talk about how shaken they are and wonder if they should report the body to the police. One takes photos. Heading out of the forest and onto the train the next morning, they all seem much more subdued. The video ends with more text warning of the forest's "negative energy" and saying that the forest is "not a tourist spot" (Tokyo DailyPhoto 2012). Though most videos do not include actual images of corpses, the other elements of this video—abandoned belongings, tape tied to trees, mentioning feelings of ominousness, low production values, and some sort of cautionary text—are all fairly common features of English-language Aokigahara videos on YouTube. These videos seem designed primarily to shock or to establish the bona fides of the person or people filming.

Through widely circulated news articles, YouTube videos, still images, and blog posts, then, an idea emerges in English-language networks of Aokigahara as a place of death and decay, of shocking body horror, of exotic otherness, and of Japan's mysterious unknowability. An important element in many of these representations is the idea of the forest as hidden, taboo, or forbidden, with the idea that the person who is shooting the video or writing the blog post is acting as an intrepid guide in a dangerous place, offering explanations and insight regarding a place that remains "other" to the viewer, bringing them close but not so close as to lose their "distant intimacy."

All of these representations of Aokigahara are filtered through the literally and figuratively small frames of the outsider seeking an authentic experience in an exotic and mysterious location: the YouTube video frame, the collection of carefully chosen images in a news story or blog post, the view captured via a smart phone camera attached to a selfie stick, and the more polished and carefully edited images revealed in a feature film. The idea of Aokigahara that emerges in English-language networks is one patched together from "the limits and multiplicities of our frames of vision," which "determine the boundaries and multiplicities of our world" (Friedberg 2006, 7). People in these networks will experience Aokigahara through these limited frames of vision, seeing a carefully curated version of the forest that will present it as scenic, frightening, mysterious, or familiar and friendly (as in videos designed to promote hiking and sightseeing in the forest). These varied ideas of Aokigahara arguably inform not only those who seek out Aokigahara-focused videos and articles but also those who create feature films set in Aokigahara. As we will see with the English-language film *The Forest*, the idea of Aokigahara as a place with an "authentic aura" can mix with creative fictions to create an exotic, othered space that reinforces the narrative of "mysterious Japan" in opposition to what has been likewise imagined as the rational, knowable "West."

SWALLOWED BY MYSTERIOUS JAPAN: *THE FOREST*

The 2016 film *The Forest* has a few surprising similarities to *Suicide Forest Village*. Both are stories of sisters dealing with the trauma of a dead parent (and with misleading memories of that parent's death). Both imagine a secret community of supernatural entities living within Aokigahara, and both culminate in one of the main characters essentially being swallowed by the forest, though in very different contexts. *The Forest* and its accompanying marketing campaign/commentary also reveal how Aokigahara—and to a certain extent Japan—are perceived by many English-language film producers. Next to *The Sea of Trees* (dir. Gus Van Sant 2015), a drama about a man from the United States who travels to Aokigahara to die, *The Forest* is arguably the most expensive and widely viewed film set in Aokigahara, featuring two fairly well-known actors and a considerable budget of USD$10 million (imdb .com 2021). It tells the story of Sarah, a young woman who journeys to Japan to find her twin sister, Jess, who supposedly went missing in Aokigahara. Jess and Sarah were raised by their grandmother after the death of their parents, supposedly at the hands of a drunk driver (though we learn later that Sarah has repressed her memories of what actually happened). With the help of an American journalist and a Japanese guide, Sarah ventures into the forest to find Jess but gradually begins to lose her mind, seeing images and people that may or may not be real. She finally kills the American journalist when she has convinced herself that he, in fact, murdered her sister. At the end of the film, Jess escapes the forest, but Sarah is literally sucked into the ground by a mass of dead hands. The last shot of the film shows the Japanese guide staring into the forest, terrified, as the camera zooms in on an image of Sarah, who has now transformed into a *yūrei*.

The Forest presents a familiar depiction of a newcomer's experience of Japan. From the beginning, Sarah is an outsider, confounded by the strange food, unfamiliar language, and bizarre behavior of the locals. In an opening scene, we cut back and forth between a flashback of Sarah at home with her husband to an image of her in a taxi in Tokyo, staring out the window. Through this narrow frame, she sees familiar fragments of Tokyo—neon-covered buildings, young women dressed in "Lolita" fashion, and a strange man who throws himself at the window of the car. She stares and is stared at: as she gawks at Tokyo, the taxi driver eyes her through the rearview mirror. Later, in a sushi restaurant, she stares at the wriggling fish that the chef cheerfully puts in front of her and then notices that the group of women next to her are staring and laughing. Japan is alien, she is an outsider, and a collection of widely circulated "outsider in Japan" images—strange food, strange fashion, language barriers, and inscrutable behavior—confirm that fact.[8] When Sarah decides to learn more about Aokigahara, she accesses it through the "virtual window" of an Internet search engine on her laptop, where a collection of images of corpses and abandoned belongings appear. Interestingly, the images on her screen are divided into the categories of "bodies," "signs," "ropes," "night," and "map," suggesting that Aokigahara can be easily broken down into a specific group of images and ideas. Later, on the train to Aokigahara, Sarah again stares out the window at the unfamiliar landscape and is stared at by a man on the train.

All of this immediately sets Sarah up in opposition to Japan and its people—she (and by extension the viewer) is the normal, rational one, and the country and people around her are inscrutable and mysterious. She stares but is also stared at, and she views everything through a literally and figuratively small frame. Her outsider status is reinforced when a Japanese guide warns Sarah and her American journalist friend, Aiden, that they may "see things" in Aokigahara, but that it is all in their heads—to which Aiden responds by sharing a smirk and a laugh with Sarah. The foreigners are the rational ones, and the Japanese are full of silly superstitions. Not surprisingly, the person that Sarah forges the closest relationship with is another foreign national—the locals exist primarily to dispense ominous warnings or exhibit unwelcoming behavior.

In the film's commentary, director Jason Zada says that Aokigahara's status as a real place was what attracted him to the project, and that he became "infatuated" with Aokigahara as he did more and more research (Zada 2016b), and yet many of the details about the forest depicted in the film are the filmmaker's invention. On a train out of Tokyo, Sarah hears a train announcement in Japanese and English that "the next stop is Aokigahara station." When she arrives at the eerily empty, mostly deserted station, the sign indeed says: "Aokigahara station" (next to a bright blue image with "Fuji Mountain" written underneath). In reality, there is no "Aokigahara station"—the closest train stations are Fuji-Yoshida and Kawaguchi-ko.[9] Sarah's journey also takes her to the fictional "Narusawa visitors' center," off a completely deserted road, which seems to double as a morgue for keeping the bodies of suicide victims. Inside, there is a large sign with "Do not leave the path" written in four different languages. As they walk through the forest, Aiden, the American journalist, tells Sarah that there are ice caves scattered beneath the forest, "whole sections that've never been explored. Some people believe it's a gateway to the other side" (Zada 2016a). In the film's commentary, director Jason Zada echoes this fiction, saying: "Actually going to the real forest, if you do run off the path, there's a good chance you'll fall down one of these [ice caves]" (Zada 2016b). (This is, needless to say, highly unlikely.)

In other words, though the creators of *The Forest* claim that the main appeal of setting a story there was the fact that Aokigahara is "a real place," the version that we see in the film is a mix of hearsay and mythology, the creation of an idea of Aokigahara based at least partly on widely circulated rumors and images sutured together from various representations on screens and in frames not unlike those that Sarah seeks out on her laptop, and inspired by the Orientalist framework of Japan as inscrutable and strange. The "real"

Aokigahara may be frightening and creepy, but for the full effect, the filmmakers felt the need to add certain embellishments that while entirely their own inventions, fit in with the Orientalist narrative about Aokigahara and "spooky Japan." The forest's "authentic aura" allows viewers to engage with it as a historical and cultural reality, even if so much else that is presented in the film is fiction.

The extent to which the film is grounded in non-Japanese perceptions of Japan as "other" comes through most strongly in the film's commentary. Director Jason Zada and producer David S. Goyer repeatedly emphasize Japan's "but also" qualities, a dynamic that goes back as far as Ruth Benedict's 1946 book *The Chrysanthemum and the Sword* (still frequently cited as an authoritative source by mainstream media, even though Benedict was never able to travel to Japan). Benedict famously wrote that "the Japanese have been described in the most fantastic series of 'but also's' ever used for any nation of the world," "polite" but also "insolent and overbearing," "submissive" but also "not easily amenable to control from above" (Benedict 2005 [1946], 1–2). These sentiments are echoed in *The Forest*'s commentary: for director Zada, Aokigahara is both "beautiful" and "a terrifying place." The ghostly figure of a schoolgirl named Hoshiko is "a sweet, innocent, lost schoolgirl one minute and then kind of this very devilish demon next time we see her" (Zada 2016b). Beyond its "but also" qualities, Japan and Aokigahara are also simply bizarre. Goyer refers to Aokigahara as an "otherworldly place in Japan," saying that transplanting a "Westerner" into that place is "very isolating and scary in and of itself." Japan is also a place that has a "culture of the supernatural" (Goyer 2016). For Zada and Goyer, then, Japan is frightening because of its dualities, and putting a "Westerner" in this place is already frightening even without the threat of vengeful spirits.

The film's imagery also emphasizes the idea of Japan as a literal black hole of other-ness, one that is easy to become consumed by, playing on the "fear of what lies beneath the enigmatic facade of Japanese aestheticism and spiritualism," the fear that "Western culture might itself be overwhelmed by the Oriental Other" (Morley and Robins 1995, 162). The film opens with a drone shot of the forest, with the camera slowly sweeping downward as small children sing an eerie song in Japanese. Before cutting away to Sarah in Japan, the camera rapidly swoops down into the forest and is enveloped in darkness. Shots of the characters within the forest during the day mostly look overcast, with dense tree growth on all sides. At one point in the film, Sarah literally falls down a black hole into one of the forest's supposedly hidden caves, where she is threatened by supernatural entities that might be all in her head. Finally, near the end of the film, when she thinks she can finally escape, she realizes that she has actually killed herself by slitting her own wrists and has become a *yūrei*. As she sinks into the forest floor, multiple black, necrotic hands reach up and pull her into the earth, echoing the film's first drone shot that plunges the viewer deep into the blackness of the forest. Aokigahara in this film is a gaping maw that literally swallows the central, non-Japanese protagonist. In the same way that various forms of Orientalism define Japan in opposition to Europe and the United States, here Aokigahara is everything that Sarah and her world are not—irrational, inscrutable, and overpowering where her own world is reasonable, understandable, and easily controlled. Where non-Japanese characters in some films set in Japan might be able to get a taste of strangeness and leave, Sarah has gotten too close, and the result is that she is overwhelmed and consumed by otherness.

The Forest is based on a fantasy image of Japan, imagining Aokigahara as a "dark space," not only in the sense that it is overgrown with trees and cut off from sunlight but also in the sense that it is cut off from the rest of the world, mysterious, and unknowable. This dark space ultimately swallows the protagonist and overwhelms her with its otherness. It is a dark version of the mythical and magical Orient, a place where the usual rules do not apply, and where one is ultimately not only repulsed by but also drawn to the all-consuming power of the forest and its malevolent spirits. The mythology that surrounds it is a combination of the filmmakers' own inventions and widely circulated images and rumors about the forest spread via YouTube videos, online journalism, and blog posts, and the forest gains its power not only from its "authentic aura"—its status as a real space and real site of death—but also from its connection to Orientalist fantasies of Japan.

CONCLUSION

The narratives of Japanese horror films and the characters/images/spaces originating in Japan that have inspired films like *Suicide Forest Village* and *The Forest* have always been connected to stories of technology and its impact on our perceptions of reality. The television and the theater screen have literally and figuratively "framed" stories of ghosts and the supernatural, and in the 2010s and beyond, we find ourselves surrounded by a multitude of large and small screens, forcing us to constantly shift our perspective (and our position as spectator or active participant). Viewing Aokigahara through these different screens and perspectives, we are able to see Orientalist visions of "exotic Japan," a tension between truth and fiction, and a space that is truly "haunted" not only by its connection to death and tragedy but also by the very spectrality of the media that records, shapes, and disseminates its narratives.

Aokigahara's place in the world of Japanese horror crosses both national and digital borders. The idea of the forest is circulated both within and outside of feature films via new media objects, things "not fixed once and for all," but which "can exist in different, potentially infinite versions" (Manovich 2001, 36). Looking again at Ōsawa Shinichi's music video shot in Aokigahara, we see a clear illustration of how Aokigahara the place, the image, the idea is formed, broken down, and reshaped for the viewer. The "real" forest is seen in darkness, a brightly lit woman with blonde hair dancing in the middle of it. But the lights and the image of the forest flicker, making it difficult sometimes to get a handle on exactly what we're seeing (Ōsawa 2010). Pieces of the forest literally break into shards, come together, and break apart again, each time presenting a slightly different view.

NOTES

1. One often-reported detail about Aokigahara is that compasses malfunction inside the forest, which is often attributed to the large amount of iron deposits in the soil (Keefe 2017). This detail adds to the forest's air of mystery, making it sound a bit like the Bermuda Triangle. In reality, compasses function normally in many parts of the forest (based on my own experience on a single trip to the forest), though some travelers have found that their compasses did not work. A 2019 post on the Fuji-Yoshida sightseeing website also argues that the "compass rumor" is not true (Fuji-Yoshida kankō 2019).

2. Such efforts include training nature guides to offer tours of the forest, offering information about hiking courses and the forest's flora and fauna, training local shopkeepers in how to recognize those who might be going into the forest to die and promoting the forest as a place of natural scenic beauty. In late 2017, the *Mainichi Shinbun* reported that interest in Aokigahara as a place of natural scenic beauty was increasing (*Mainichi Shinbun* 2017). Efforts to promote the forest's scenic beauty also seem to have the goal of raising the overall tourism numbers, given that a generally larger population of hikers and sightseers in the forest is likely to deter anyone seeking to end their life in solitude.

3. In January 2018, YouTube star Logan Paul filmed himself and a group of friends gawking at a corpse hanging from a tree in Aokigahara. Though the video was taken down hours after it was posted, it garnered several million views and inspired outrage both inside and outside Japan for Paul's insensitivity, leading him to issue an apology. The video also led to a great deal of reporting on both Aokigahara and "toxic" YouTube culture (Kidwell 2018; Romano 2018; Dodds 2018). By March 2020, an image of Paul was still one of the first images to appear in a Google search for "suicide forest."

4. This video was perhaps inspired by a story connected to another famous location for suicides in Japan—the Tōjinbō Cliffs, located on the Sea of Japan in Fukui Prefecture. In 2016, it was reported that the large numbers of people playing Pokemon Go near the cliffs had led to a reduction in suicides, which led at least one forum commenter to say, "Next, Mt. Fuji's sea of trees!" (Livedoor News 2016).

5. Though likely helped by a lack of competition (the film was released in February 2020, just before many Japanese movie theaters shut down for a lengthy period due to COVID-19), *Howling Village* did surprisingly well at the box office in Japan, bringing in approximately 12.5 million dollars and ranking sixteenth out of all films screening in Japanese theaters in 2020 (Box Office Mojo 2021).

6. *Nihonjinron* (theories of Japanese-ness) refers to a set of pseudoscientific ideas about Japanese uniqueness that includes writing on culture, biology, language, and psychology. For more see Yoshino Kosaku's *Cultural Nationalism in Japan: A Sociological Inquiry* (1992).

7. While it is true that Japan's suicide rate is one of the highest in the world, particularly among industrialized nations (Ōtake 2017), Francesca DiMarco argues that the "glorification of the values of honor and self-sacrifice in the discourse on suicide" is in fact a "glorification of Japanese otherness" that has been emphasized both by Japanese and non-Japanese media (DiMarco 2016, 181). English-language reporting on Aokigahara often mentions the "lack of taboo" surrounding suicide as one of the reasons for Japan's high overall suicide rate and the large number of suicides in Aokigahara. Popular representations of samurai in the United States, from the TV series *Shogun* (1980) to the film *The Last Samurai* (2003), also frequently focus on *seppuku* and the idea of "honorable death" by suicide.

8. These depictions of encounters with strange fashion, food, or behavior in Japan can be easily found in "only in Japan" YouTube videos, but they also appear in numerous movies that depict foreign nationals in Japan, including *Mr. Baseball* (1992), *Black Rain* (1989), *Lost in Translation* (2003), and *The Ramen Girl* (2008), helping to establish the foreign character as the rational/normal one and the surrounding Japanese people as strange or "other."

9. Bloomfield (2018) notes that *The Forest* was shot in Serbia, arguing that the Serbian forest "takes the place of Aokigahara, a substitute for the actual forest in much the same way that mediated images are substitutes for the viewer's phsyical presence and Sara is the substitute for the audience. Viewers get the impression that the forest represented is Aokigahara, marveling at its beauty while misinformed about its authenticity" (164).

Chapter 4

From *Ringu* to *Rings*
Porous Screens and Virtual Windows in the Later **Ringu** Films

In Koma Natsumi's short 2019 comic *Sadako at the End of the World* (*Shūmatsu no Sadako-san*), the *Ringu* series' vengeful girl-spirit with the long black hair takes on the unusual role of playmate to two other children. The setting is postapocalyptic, and young girls Ai and Hī have been surviving on their own for a while. When Sadako, who communicates via an iPad, emerges from their TV screen, they're mostly happy to have a new playmate. Sadako, for her part, is eager to find more people to curse, though this may prove difficult in a massively depopulated world. "When the people are gone, the curses will be gone too," Sadako thinks. "Will I finally disappear too?" (Koma 2019, 108). But after cursing the two young children—in a decidedly compassionate way—Sadako finds herself still present in the world. She wonders if someone else is still alive. In a short series of comic frames, she turns her face, still obscured by her hair, toward us, the readers, and says: "There you are" (*a, ita*) (Koma 2019, 120). The last page of the comic is an image of Sadako with her hands positioned on the edges of a single frame, making to climb out of it toward us, the words "there you are" superimposed over the long, black hair that hangs over her face.

Sadako has spent decades climbing out of different screens and frames and moving between different platforms and narratives since she was first introduced in Suzuki Kōji's 1991 novel *Ringu* (*The Ring*, which would eventually be expanded to five novels). She has been depicted in comic books both serious and humorous, in multiple Japanese films and television shows/miniseries, in two U.S. remakes and one spin-off film, and in one Korean remake (*The Ring Virus*, 1999, dir. Kim Dong-bin). In various commercials and publicity stunts, she has appeared on Instagram, as a group of dancers in a heavy metal music video, on the side of giant advertising trucks moving through Shibuya, as a collection of stickers on the LINE chat app, in commercials encouraging patrons to practice good movie theater manners, and as the subject of a satirical *seiken hōsō* (election broadcast), part of a promotional campaign for *Sadako vs. Kayako* (dir. Shiraishi Kōji 2016), in which she competed for the title of scariest ghost. In the late 2010s, her presence shifted back and forth from terrifying to cuddly, not only appearing in her usual form in films like *Sadako vs. Kayako* and *Sadako* (dir. Nakata Hideo 2019) but also existing as a sort of parody of herself—never showing her face, moving awkwardly, and occasionally struggling to make sense of her role in the world. At one point in *Sadako at the End of the World*, an older woman that Sadako and the young girls encounter seems to realize that Sadako is not of this world. "A story with no one to continue it is the same as no story at all," the older woman says. "What kind of story are you telling, magic girl?" (Koma 2019, 70) In the late 2010s and beyond, at least, more than a few people and institutions seem to be invested in continuing Sadako's story, moving her between platforms, screens, and universes in much the same way as she moves between media devices within her narratives. As with so many Japanese horror stories in the late 2010s and beyond, *how* Sadako's story is told has changed significantly, and the manner of its telling has influenced our perception of Sadako and the world that she inhabits. New media objects and devices naturally play a part in both how Sadako's story is shared and within the narratives of her films.

How has Sadako's relationship to both new and old media changed since her film debut in 1998, and how has the production and marketing of the *Ringu* films changed to acknowledge *Ringu* audiences' new relationships to certain kinds of media devices and platforms? In their focus on a multitude of large and small screens, how have the later *Ringu* sequels and remakes reinforced the omnipresence of "virtual windows" in our everyday lives? How do the many screens and digital interfaces that Sadako moves through exist as semipermeable barriers, "a *mise en abyme* of representation" (Friedberg 2006, 109)? Not surprisingly, later films like *Sadako 3D* (2012, dir. Hanabusa Tsutomu), *Sadako*, and the U.S.-made *Rings* (2017, dir. F. Javier Gutiérrez) shift the focus from VCRs, TVs, and video cassettes to YouTube, Niconico, and digital copying. Beyond the use of smart phones, computers, and online streaming platforms as vessels for Sadako to enact her revenge, these films also focus more generally on the role that social media, digital video, and streaming play in the characters' everyday lives. In some cases, the film's paratexts—publicity stunts, trailers, fake commercials, Instagram campaigns—also reveal the ways that new media objects and devices are central to the way that audiences engage with these films. Sadako in the later *Ringu* films pulls us *into* the screen rather than causing us to tilt our head back from it (Galloway 2012, 12).[1] She illustrates the layered and leveled construction of the interface, revealing that "the social field itself constitutes a grand interface, an interface between subject and world, between surface and source, and between critique and the objects of criticism" (Galloway, 2012, 54).

In this chapter, I will examine the genesis and evolution of the *Ringu* films, beginning with Nakata Hideo's *Don't Look Up* (*Joyūrei*, 1996), which laid the groundwork for many of the images and story elements depicted in *Ringu*, examining screenwriters/film scholars Konaka Chiaki and Takashi Hiroshi's perspectives on the development of *Ringu* and its place in the world of J-horror. I argue that *Ringu* and *Don't Look Up* make use not only of frames-within-frames but also with media objects embedded in other media objects (*Don't Look Up*, for example, is the story of a mysterious piece of film footage that appears in the celluloid of footage from a more current film). I will then focus on three post-2010 *Ringu* films: *Sadako 3D, Sadako,* and *Rings*, which reveal the extent to which the character of Sadako has moved beyond the realm of television/VCRs and into the realm of computers, smartphones, and streaming platforms like Niconico. With their focus on a variety of "virtual windows," all of these films reveal the permeable nature of the digital screen, a frame, and a window that pulls us into the world of the film in the same moment that it reflects our own image back at us.

FROM *DON'T LOOK UP* TO *RINGU* AND BEYOND

As Alexander Zahlten (2017) and Steven T. Brown (2018) have documented, *Ringu*, by far the most successful and well-known J-horror film, based its aesthetic on the cheap, bare bones structure of TV programs like the *True Scary Stories* (*Hontō ni atta kowai hanashi*) series (Zahlten 2017, 163; Brown 2018, 2). The film and its sequels, prequels, remakes, and offshoots center around an invented urban legend of a cursed video—watch it and you will die, though the manner and time of your death varies from film to film. The video is the psychic creation of Sadako, a young girl whose mother had psychic powers but was attacked as a fake. Sadako was also gifted with psychic/telekinetic abilities and was thrown into a well to die by her father. The video is a manifestation of her rage. The only way to escape its curse is to copy the video and show it to someone else, effectively ensuring that Sadako's rage will spread throughout the world, endlessly duplicated.

Though *Ringu* is often seen as the genesis of the J-horror genre, Kinoshita Chika notes that another point of origin can be found in *Psychic Vision* (discussed in chapter 2), a short, straight-to-video film about the ghost of a woman that appears repeatedly in video footage, audio recordings, and photographs (Kinoshita 2009, 235 n.31). Another precursor to *Ringu* is Nakata's *Don't Look Up*, which also deals with the ghost of an actress who seems to be haunting not only a film studio but also the actual film reels being used to shoot a new movie. *Ringu*, *Psychic Vision*, and *Don't Look Up* all deal with similar themes and questions: ghost photographs, haunting by vengeful female spirits, found media objects, and the inherent spectrality of film, photography, and certain types of media and media devices. While arguably only *Psychic Vision* could be called a found footage horror film, all of these films are really about found footage, and about collecting pieces of media to try to make sense of the whole. Often, though, the "record" of events under examination leads to more questions than answers.

In a 2021 video conversation with Colleen Laird, Kinoshita Chika noted that photography and film have always existed as "a means to overcome death" (Laird 2021), preserving images of people and things that will live on long after their real-world referents have passed away or fallen into ruin. Like *Toshimaen: The Movie* (discussed in chapter 1), *Don't Look Up* is in many ways a record of a vanished world. The movie was filmed at the empty Nikkatsu studios just after the production company had gone bankrupt (which saw director Nakata facing an uncertain future) (Mes and Sharp 2005, 255). The film exists in a time of transition, when larger studios were in decline and smaller films made for the video market were becoming more common. Frequent shots of empty World War II-era sets and dark rafters already feel ghostly. In the film, a director, Murai, is shooting a World War II drama when, during viewings of the daily rushes, he discovers old footage of an actress mixed in with footage of his film. Kinoshita describes this sequence as one that "crystallizes J-horror's take on terror, temporality, and archive, at the genre's genesis" (Kinoshita 2009, 113). The director is sure he has seen the actress before, on a TV program that he watched as a child, but other crew members claim that the footage is from a film that was never released. In this sense, Kinoshita argues, the film's Japanese title (which translates to "ghost actress"), is misleading: "the film is not about the ghost of an actress. Not a horrible story behind the surface of the celluloid, but the lack thereof and the surface itself, generate terror" (Kinoshita 2009, 114). A film that never existed and a lack of material presence. A ghostly image of a woman in white also appears in this mysterious footage, and there are rumors of a woman in white seen in the rafters of the studio. The younger actress in the film falls to her death, and ghostly images pop-up on newer film footage. The film ends with a malevolent presence in the form of a woman in white attacking the director, and a final scene seems to hint that perhaps she has now possessed another actress.

Don't Look Up screenwriter Takahashi Hiroshi, who had worked with Nakata on the *True Scary Stories* TV series, writes that film—and horror films in particular—are very much about the tension between seen and unseen: how much to show or not to show and the terror of revealing something that is supposed to remain hidden (Takahashi 2004, 37). He claims that the inspiration for *Don't Look Up* came from his own experience of seeing a ghostly image on TV when he was a child, comparing it to other examples of "films that shouldn't exist," like the one in Tanizaki Junichiro's short story "The Tumor with a Human Face," which tells the story of an actress who appeared in a film but has no memory of shooting it (Takahashi 2004, 33). In *Don't Look Up*, this "film that shouldn't exist" literally invades the material elements of another film, "infecting" it in the manner that Sadako's cursed videotape would eventually spread its curse, and in the way that "haunted" audio equipment, cameras, video footage, and photographs bring harm to the characters of *Psychic Vision*. *Don't Look Up* also, like *Ringu* and its later iterations, displays many different forms of "haunted media," from stories of a TV program that couldn't have existed to corrupted film reels to paper photographs. In one scene, a paper photograph of the lead actress in the film that director Murai is shooting suddenly comes to life, accompanied by jarring music. The photograph then shifts to a grainy, black-and-white image of the ghostly woman that appeared in the old film footage. Later, after the director has been attacked by the ghostly presence and mysteriously disappeared, the assistant director and the lead actress search his apartment for clues. The assistant finds the paper photograph, but holes have been ripped in the eyes. The lead actress is behaving strangely, her affect noticeably different. In the final shot, we see her reflection as she stares into a mirror and says: "He must have wandered off somewhere" (Nakata 1996). Images of this actress and the other ghostly female image in the film are constantly presented to us through a further veil of mediation: as photographs on a wall, as reflections in a mirror, or as grainy images in celluloid.

 The ghost in *Don't Look Up* seems to jump easily between photographs, celluloid, and even the real world. She haunts old film reels that are used to make a new film, and thus ends up infecting not only the physical materials used to shoot the film but also the entire film shoot itself. She seems to possess a paper photograph, and at the end of the film, we are left to wonder if she has now possessed the body of the lead actress in the film (an illusion of whom the director saw just before he was attacked). Like Sadako, the ghostly woman manifests in media objects that cause harm to anyone who comes in contact with them, and also directly kills people in the real world (it is rumored that she may have pushed an actress to her death years before, she seems to have pushed the younger actress Saori to her death during the present film shoot, and by the end of the film it seems that she has killed the director and possessed the lead actress). Though we never learn the root cause of her anger, like Sadako, she seems to manifest as ambiguously directed rage.

 In its frequent shifts in perspective, *Don't Look Up* also underscores the tension between different media types that will be even more apparent in later *Ringu* sequels, remakes, and offshoots. The film opens with eerie music playing over images of what appear to be life-size dolls in a traditional Japanese home, but then director Murai's face enters the frame, and we see that this is a model set, the dolls being used to plan for how the actors will be positioned in scenes from the film-within-the-film. Many scenes show us this film being shot, with images of staff setting up cameras and recording equipment. Frequently, though, we are transported to the world of the film-within-the film, set during World War II, with those scenes filling the entire screen—only to cut away suddenly to the mysterious footage of the "film that shouldn't exist," which is now mixed in with the current film's footage.[2] We frequently hear the noise of film reels turning on projectors or within cameras, or the rattling sound of a damaged film reel. As viewers, we move back and forth between watching a film set during World War II, watching that film being made, and watching footage that "should not exist" of a dead actress and the ghostly presence behind her.

With *Ringu*, Takahashi and Nakata would collaborate again to create a story of a cursed media object, a ghostly woman with long black hair (and wearing a white dress), and the idea of a video that should not exist (and is dangerous to view). Like *Don't Look Up*, *Ringu* is also shrouded in shadow—indoor scenes are dimly lit (or lit only by the glow of a television screen). The film is also a lengthy series of encounters with obsolete media devices. Beyond the VCR and videocassette, characters are shown repeatedly answering landline phones. Journalist Asakawa Reiko asks her ex-husband Ryūji to take a photo of her with a Polaroid camera. Photographs of Sadako's victims are dropped off at a photo shop and picked up later, after they have been developed. Reiko and Ryūji examine the cursed videotape on a large, clunky machine with oversized knobs. The speed at which 1990s media moved impacts the film's pacing. Waiting for photo film to be developed, traveling somewhere to acquire a physical copy of the video cassette, finding and using a different machine to copy the cassette—all of these actions take considerably more time than their equivalent actions would in the 2010s and beyond.

In the production of *Ringu*, Nakata also made use of fairly simple and cheap "analog" visual effects. Takahashi notes that in the famous scene of Sadako emerging from the television set, the footage was played backward, the goal being to give Sadako's movements an otherworldly feel (Takahashi 2004, 36). The effect is indeed striking and has informed much of Sadako's movement in her other appearances in films and other video-based paratexts (including in her promotional "election broadcast" video, in which the actress playing her silently moves her shoulders and arms in an eerie imitation of Sadako's movements). Konaka and Takahashi have both argued that the "central problem" of horror is how to represent the ghost on screen, with Takahashi expressing frustration that ghosts are almost always played by human actors, and that is a challenge to make them look not-human (Takashi 2004, 26–27; Konaka 2003, 114–122). As Kinoshita notes, Takahashi offers a list of techniques for representing the ghost, including not showing the ghost's face and making its movements "nonhuman" (Kinoshita 2009, 115). Takahashi and Nakata clearly followed these rules in their depiction of Sadako, and yet Takahashi claimed to be "dissatisfied" with the result, partly because Sadako still looked human, and partly because they took the "safe" route and showed her face . . . but not all of it, only her single, staring eye. In choosing to "reveal" the film's ghost, Takahashi believed, the filmmakers had also revealed her inherent humanness (Takahashi 2004, 37).

Revealed and hidden, real and unreal, mediated and unmediated—these tensions are at the heart of *Ringu*'s lasting appeal. Kristen Lacefield writes that *Ringu* connects us to "the dichotomy of simultaneous connection and discomfort" that "lies at the heart of the human subject's relation to media technology" (Lacefield 2010, 2). Technology like TV is intimate—in many homes in the late 1950s and beyond, the TV became a sort of replacement for the hearth—but its "electronic presence" (Sconce 2000) also produces a sense of discomfort. Jeffrey Sconce argues that *Ringu* is less a "haunted TV" film and more a "harbinger of a new paradigm in horror, one that would abandon the discorporative fantasies attending wireless infinity in favor of the more targeted terrors of viral transmission" (Sconce 2010, 216). *Ringu* associates "ubiquitous technological mediation" with "the intrusion of 'posthuman' otherness into contemporary cultural life" (White 2005, 41). Like other representative examples of J-horror, Ringu "draw(s) on the media saturated environment in contemporary Japan in order to activate the uncanny, making supernatural apparitions through technologies of mechanical reproduction and electronic communications in the living room" (Kinoshita 2009, 106). In *Ringu*, as in *Don't Look Up* and *Psychic Vision*, intangible ghosts are made tangible through media technology, and that which "should not exist" is brought into existence through cameras, TVs, and VCRs. Though her work focuses primarily on the novelization of *Ringu* and not the film, Raechel Dumas brilliantly builds on many of these analyses of "media anxiety" in *Ringu* to argue for the "simulacratic specter not as a confirmation of nonidentity, but rather as an attempt to grapple with the possibility of a postmodern ontology that is grounded in the rise of the technological" (Dumas 2018, 49). Sadako's spectral existence, endlessly mediated and copied "(resists) through repetition the interpellation of her identity into an overdetermined narrative of victimization, vengeance, and resolution" (50). Her "repetition with a difference" (Braidotti 2011, 110) is not mindless copying, but active resistance. She is part of a film that should not exist, but her rage multiplies across platforms and devices, mutating as it moves, impossible to ignore.

Though the first *Ringu* film itself was made before smart phones, tablets, and personal computers were widespread—before many of us were surrounded by multitude of screens/windows—it is still a vivid example of the effective use of frame/screen "layering" in J-horror, both within the narrative itself and in the manner of the film's dissemination. Maekawa Osamu and Mitsuyo Wada-Marciano note that Japanese horror films have frequently made use of frames-within-frames. Wada-Marciano writes that in *Ringu*'s sequence of the cursed videotape, the film "carefully overlaps the frame of the television screen with that of the film itself. The gaze of the character in the film thus completely overlaps with the camera's gaze and then the audience's as well . . . . The whole scheme creates the illusion that the film itself is the medium transmitting the curse" (Wada-Marciano 2012, 34). Maekawa, building on Wada-Marciano, adds that a further frame "layer" exists in J-horror's origins in video, and in the way that it was circulated via information in young people's phones, online reviews, and rental videos, arguing that "the medium frame exists inside and outside of the movie frame" (Maekawa 2015, 12). Given that the only way to beat the curse is to copy the tape and show it to someone else, "the *Ring* virus itself resembles the very processes of textual translation it so gleefully spawns . . . Horror adapts; like a virus, it goes on and on" (Stringer 2007, 304).

Further, when considering the video tape, we must remember that replaying it causes degradation of image quality, which adds to the eerie quality of the images (Maekawa 2015, 15). The image of "snow" on a video tape is both an image itself and a link to the video's production process, revealing that the boundaries between inside/outside, in-frame/outside-of-frame, and move world/real world are porous (15). The absence of an image is also an image in itself—as Kinoshita argues, film is "always punctuated by the absence of the image itself" (Laird 2021), given that there are always "gaps" in the twenty-four frames per second that the spectator's eye sees. "There is always a moment," Kinoshita says, "when there is no image" (Laird 2021). Maekawa notes that video replay produces not only deterioration but also "gaps" in the video footage, similar to the strange interruptions that appear in the film stock used in *Don't Look Up*. It is in these spaces that ghosts often appear, and audiences feel that they must be on the lookout for ghosts appearing in these "gaps" (Maekawa 2015, 11).

Looking at *Ringu* and *Don't Look Up*, then, we can see the importance not only of frames-within-frames (both within the narratives of the films themselves and in the manner in which they were viewed and disseminated) but also of the empty spaces that are an inevitable product of the film production process. In *Don't Look Up*, these "gaps" and disruptions in the physical celluloid are infected with a ghostly presence that goes on to infect the entire film production process, ultimately killing two people (and possibly possessing another). In *Ringu*, Sadako's curse is transmitted through replication of a video tape, which naturally leads to degradation of video quality and images of static and distortion that intensify the ghostly feeling of the video and also point to its origins. Though both of these films were released in a much less screen-saturated world, they still managed to layer multiple windows and frames to produce a "sense of the horrific (that) derives from the idea that a curse is disseminated through transmedia" (Wada-Marciano 2012, 34). Viewed today, their images and technology may seem quaint, but the horror of the endlessly mediated image, the endless copy that degrades and mutates but still curses, remains.

SADAKO 3D, *SADAKO*, AND *RINGS*: THROUGH THE VIRTUAL WINDOW

In the years since *Ringu*, its sequels/prequels, and its first U.S. remakes (*The Ring* [2002, dir. Gore Verbinski] and *The Ring Two* [2005, dir. Nakata Hideo]) were released, Sadako has continued to appear in films, manga, parody videos, and publicity stunts in Japan and around the world.[3] Much of this is thanks to the Kadokawa Corporation, the massive media conglomerate that published Suzuki Kōji's *Ringu* novels, had a hand in producing the first *Ringu* film, and continues to produce *Ringu* sequels and offshoots, as well as publishing humorous manga featuring the character of Sadako. As they have done since the late 1970s, Kadokawa have produced and distributed *Ringu*-related content as part of a "media mix" model, "a package of print media, film, and music marketed by a single company to the widest possible audience, with each product advertising the others" (Zahlten 2017, 102). In the 1970s and 1980s, Kadokawa "went from selling a film to selling something that is much less specific to its medium, which at this stage was a specific narrative embedded in spectacle" (Zahlten 2017, 103). To critics, the films produced under this model were all spectacle and no depth, "a self-referential commodity thus decentered the filmic text and narrative in particular," sometimes defined as *imēji-ka* (becoming-image), or "a shift to surface spectacle away from narrative substance and politics" (Zahlten 2017, 107). The later *Ringu* films produced by Kadokawa, including *Sadako vs. Kayako*, *Sadako 3D*, *Sadako 3D 2*, and *Sadako*, arguably fit this model of selling "a specific narrative embedded in . . . spectacle." The advertising push is also very apparent: in a paperback edition of the humorous manga *Sadako-san and Sadako-chan* (*Sadako-san to Sadako-chan*, Tsutsumi Aya 2019), the comic's obi[4] includes an advertisement for the 2019 *Sadako* film *and* for Suzuki Kōji's novel *Tide* (also published by Kadokawa), on which the film *Sadako* is very loosely based. In *Sadako 3D*, the story begins with a cursed Niconico video

(Kadokawa formed a capital alliance with Dwango Corporation, the operator of Niconico, in 2011, and the two companies merged in 2014 [FISCO Ltd. 2017]). The many incarnations of Sadako produced in the 2010s and beyond, then, show the influence of the Kadokawa model and the presence of the Kadokawa Corporation not only in their marketing and dissemination but also within the narratives of the films themselves.

The later *Ringu* sequels and remakes also reveal the extent to which Sadako's form has mutated, now moving easily between a multitude of screens and digital environments that are a constant background presence in the everyday lives of both the films' characters and audiences. Frames, walls, mirrors, screens, and windows all provide a view into different worlds, projecting outward and pulling us in, offering a view but also altering that view. Public and private, inside and outside—imagining Friedberg's virtual windows in the late 2010s and beyond, we see the way that certain forms of new media and their digital screens "call into question the separation between publicity and privacy," the way they render users "curiously inside out . . . private subjects exposed in public" (Chun 2016b, 12). These screens frame a film's characters and our own viewing experiences. They reflect the character's faces and our own, not only pushing outward with a 3D technology but also inviting us to fall inward, into the virtual window that frames a view of a separate world.

The notions of layers of reality/authenticity, spatially and temporally fractured frames, and the constant sharing/circulation of new media objects discussed throughout this book are illustrated vividly in the later *Ringu* sequels and remakes. Where the early *Ringu* films featured frames-within-frames and media-within-media, these later films present those images and motifs in the context of an even more heavily mediated world, one in which we are much more likely to watch these films on portable media devices or computers. As with *Suicide Forest Village* and *Toshimaen: The Movie*'s frequent shifts between camera phone footage, live video-streaming footage, and the images of the films themselves, the later *Ringu* films feature frequent movement between screens/devices and frequent shifts in perspective that further "fracture" the sense of reality/authenticity created in the films.

Like *Toshimaen: The Movie*, *Sadako 3D* exists at the nexus of many different media types. Made with a theatrical 3D audience in mind and abounding in 3D gimmicks, the film appears to be part of an overall effort to draw audiences into movie theaters in a time when theater attendance had declined (though it would see a significant increase in the 2010s [MPAJ 2021]). The film's narrative, however, centers on digital media. *Sadako 3D* opens with a Niconico video, this one a live broadcast that appears to show Kashiwada Seiji, an artist, dying by suicide. We learn that Kashiwada was bullied online and seeks to "resurrect" Sadako to enact vengeance. As usual, the narrative centers around different characters' efforts to escape the curse after watching the video or to solve the mystery so that others will not become victims. Where previous *Ringu* stories might have centered on a physical video cassette and its copies, now the tension arises from the idea that, in theory, nothing ever truly vanishes from the Internet. As characters search for the "cursed video" in question, one net-savvy character notes that Niconico deletes certain video content from the public site, but erased content still remains on the Niconico server (and can still linger elsewhere on the Internet via copies). In both this film and its sequel, characters are often shown smashing physical objects like laptops and smartphones as a way to eliminate the cursed video footage, but of course the objects no longer matter—the curse exists in the cloud, ephemeral but easily transferred from one device to another.

From the very beginning, *Sadako 3D* emphasizes the layering of frames and perspectives, simultaneously showing us the many ways that a "cursed" Niconico video is consumed. In the beginning of the film, as Kashiwada Seiji sets the scene for a video of his own suicide, the camera focuses on a smartphone screen, which contains an image of the chair that he will sit in. We then cut to a timer counting down to the live broadcast and the image of another man's reflection in his own home computer screen, preparing to watch the video. Next, a woman's reflection, watching her screen as she wraps the cord around her hairdryer. Next, a man in flannel snacking as he watches, an anime figurine on his desk. Finally, an image of what this man sees: Kashiwada sitting in the chair, the video frame still flanked by anime figurines on the other man's desk. We watch the characters, they watch themselves, we watch their reflections in their digital screens, and if we are watching on a computer, we might see our own reflection on the surface of a screen.[5] Text comments scroll across the screen in Niconico fashion, recalling the endless blocks of text and "scrolling stories" encountered on 2channel, and then, jarringly, the camera—and we—dive *into* the computer screen, through lines of pixelation, right up to Kashiwada's face. Kashiwada says "Well, let's begin" (*sa, hajimeyō*) (Hanabusa 2012).

The opening scene of Kashiwada's live video broadcast begins with almost all of the participants—the characters in the film and we, the spectators—viewing things from the outside, the reflection of human faces layered over the virtual windows of home computer screens that exist very much as habitual objects (figure 4.1). These screens provide an incidental background for people who are blow-drying their hair, snacking, or just watching a random video before going to bed. In the case of a man eating snacks, the computer is likely one of many frames through which he consumes narratives (given the presence of the anime figurines, we can assume that the man likely reads a lot of manga). The faint glow of the computer screen in the darkness has replaced the glow of the TV set from the original *Ringu* film, which had long

Figure 4.1 A man's face is reflected in his computer screen as he watches a live video broadcast in *Sadako 3D* (**Hanabusa Tsutomu 2012**). *Source*: Screenshot taken by author.

since replaced the glow of the fireplace. These images remind us of the ways that both the consumption and sharing of scary stories has changed—within the narrative of the film itself, characters gather around the equivalent of a virtual campfire, waiting for a video to appear in their personal screens. As viewers, meanwhile, we may be not only watching all of this play out in a theater, or may be watching it on our own personal screen at home, drawn into the world of the film but also seeing our own reflections mixed in with the reflections of the characters.

But then, when the camera punches through the virtual window of the computer screen, projecting us through lines of pixelation and into Kashiwada's video, moving right up to the edge of his face, suddenly we are no longer passive observers. We—and the characters watching the video within the film—have fallen through the frame and are now within the video. Just as Ōtani Rinka's "Akkīna" was able to "fly out of the screen" and move from the *Suicide Forest Village* narrative to the "real" world of a promotional video, so we and the characters watching the video in *Sadako 3D* are able to shift our perspectives, an effect that would surely be magnified when viewing the film in 3D in a theater. *Sadako 3D* may not be a virtual reality experience, but it calls to mind the question that Anne Friedberg posed at the end of *The Virtual Window*: "Is there a new logic to vision as our windows, frames, screens are ever more fractured and virtually multiplied? Which technologies will break through the frame and have us climb through the virtual window?" (Friedberg 2006, 242) Along with this early scene of the camera traveling directly into the frame of the computer screen, in *Sadako 3D* we see multiple examples of a hand literally reaching out of a screen and toward the audience (another image enhanced when viewed in 3D). We fall into the screen and what is within the screen reaches out to us, and in the next scene, an actual media device becomes a projectile. We see a man sitting at a bus stop becoming increasingly agitated as he watches something on his laptop (presumably the video we have just seen). He stands up and walks into traffic, where he is immediately hit and killed by a truck. His laptop flies out of his hands and toward us—another 3D effect that has an actual frame/screen almost flying out of our frame of viewing. An actual media device potentially flying out of another one, and possibly even a computer flying out of a computer screen, given how many films are viewed via a computer.

The ubiquity of certain technologies and the nature of Internet-based pop-up images and advertising also make it much more difficult to avoid a cursed video. The "red room" curse depicted in one of the *2channel Curse* feature films (discussed in chapter 1) was predicated on the fact that in the 1990s and 2000s, it was common to encounter pop-up windows, particularly on websites with questionable content. These pop-ups were hard to get rid of, and clicking on them could often infect one's computer with malware, or result in even more popups appearing all over the screen. In a later scene in *Sadako 3D*, the cursed Niconico video of Kashiwada Seiji's suicide pops up unbidden on main character Takanori's computer. He and his girlfriend Akane frantically try to close the window and turn off the computer—we see their hands rapidly pushing buttons on the computer keyboard. The images of Kashiwada on the screen multiply until we see a dozen images of the same video layered over each other, not unlike the dreaded image of rapidly multiplying error message windows common in the 1990s when applications like Internet Explorer would crash. Akane and Takanori desperately try to stop the video, but the images continue to multiply across the computer screen. Finally, the screen goes black, Takanori is blasted backward by some sort of force emanating from the screen, and then Sadako's hand reaches out to grip Akane's neck. Takanori and Akane run from the apartment, but the evil is not so easily evaded, given the presence of so many random screens in everyday life. When Takanori and Akane rush outside, they are immediately confronted with images of Sadako on a wall of TV screens outside a store. Then, Sadako appears in a video positioned on the side of a giant truck, a type of advertising promotion seen frequently in major shopping areas like Shibuya and Shinjuku (and one that has actually been used to promote several *Ringu* sequels). As Akane watches, Sadako's hair reaches out, wraps itself around Takanori, and pulls him into the truck's video screen. Again and again, characters in the film—and those of us watching it—are presented with objects flying out of screens, or that seem to fall into them.

Sadako 3D also quickly sets up a feeling of tension between old and new media, shown primarily through the presence of two policemen: a younger, somewhat digital-savvy cop named Nakamura, and an older cop, Koiso, who is hostile to the Internet and digital technology in general. When Nakamura begins to explain to Koiso the story of the cursed video, Koiso quickly cuts him off, telling him that good cops shouldn't do their investigating on the Internet, they should do it on foot. When they discover that Kashiwada, who created the video, was a popular online artist with a large following who was attacked by an online mob, Koiso shouts that he "couldn't understand half" of what Nakamura described (Hanabusa 2012). He sneers at the idea that a video could cause someone to commit suicide: "Is the computer poisonous?" (Hanabusa 2012). (It clearly is in *Sadako 3D*, though perhaps not in the way that Koiso imagines.) Teacher Akane, too, is worried about how much her students use smartphones. Where the original *Ringu* video was passed via videotaped copies, this new *noroi no dōga* (cursed video) is easily found online. In class, student Noriko searches for it and seems to find it, but her first attempts result in a "404 not found" message, and then in a prank video of snails. Later, teacher Akane tells her not to visit "weird websites" and Noriko simply waves a cheerful farewell, clearly unconcerned with this danger. Later, she does find the video, and Sadako's hand reaches out to her through her phone screen. As Noriko crashes through her bedroom window and plummets to the ground, her cell phone hovers just above her, falling together in a sea of fragments of broken glass (Hanabusa 2012). Present throughout the film is the idea that young people are vulnerable to the temptations of "weird" digital media objects accessed through their phones, and that they have lost touch with old-fashioned skills (like the ability to do police work on foot rather than via the Internet).

This sense of tension between old and new media also plays out in the depiction of streaming platforms and how young people use them. Like *Toshimaen: The Movie*, other *Ringu* sequels seem to feel a sense of caution and moralization toward new media technologies like YouTube, Niconico, and the desire to achieve fame and fortune by posting ever more outrageous video content. In the 2019 film *Sadako*, directed by original *Ringu* director Nakata Hideo, a young female doctor, Mayu, encounters a child who may be Sadako reborn, and the film follows her quest to save the child and break the curse. We learn that Mayu and her brother, Kazuma, were abandoned as children and raised in foster care. Kazuma is trying to gain fame as a YouTuber who specializes in physical comedy, much to his sister's chagrin. Much of *Sadako*'s media anxiety, then, is focused on Japan's YouTube culture that rewards reckless behavior and "prank" videos. Surveys conducted since the mid-2000s have consistently ranked "professional YouTuber" as a popular career choice for young boys (survey results released in 2021 ranked it at number 2, behind "company employee" but ahead of "soccer player" and "game creator" [Yahoo! Japan 2021]). In the case of *Sadako*, Kazuma has created an alter ego called "Fantastic Kazuma" whose videos bear a resemblance to popular Japanese YouTube videos featuring wacky pranks and physical comedy. Mayu first encounters one of his videos in the hospital, where a group of children are watching it on a tablet. When she confronts Kazuma, he tells her that this has been his dream since he was a child and that it is now the number one career dream of children. She remains skeptical.

Importantly, we learn that in this film's version of the "cursed video" story, a mysterious video appeared online at some point and pieces of it gradually came to be mixed with other online videos. The people who made and uploaded those videos are then cursed—Sadako has "infected" them and their videos digitally, producing cursed videos-within-videos, not unlike the analog film-within-a-film that appeared in *Don't Look Up*. This, apparently, is what happened to Kazuma and the videos that he uploaded. Where copying the video tapes in the original *Ringu* films required a certain amount of agency, now the cursed footage seems to simply exist, randomly "infecting" videos uploaded by YouTubers (earlier in the film we see the same staticky image of a skull in the middle of a prank "pickup artist" video that other YouTubers have recorded). Ghosts can enter through the digital gaps in the cursed video footage, just as they entered the "gaps" in celluloid in *Joyūrei*, in the cursed video cassette of the original *Ringu*, and in the background of image and sound recordings in *Psychic Vision*. This empty space, a space that seems easily filled with ghosts, recalls the empty spaces within the cinematic medium itself, the material *absence* that Kinoshita notes exists within any film (Laird 2021). J-horror is part of "a long tradition of film theory that shows particular fascination with the photo-based film's ability to render the living and the dead" (Kinoshita 2009, 114). In the case of *Sadako*, ghosts take advantage of the "gaps" in much-copied digital videos, easily filling these empty spaces and spreading their presence throughout the online world.

The humorous manga *Sadako-san and Sadako-chan*, released at the same time as the *Sadako* film, focuses even more on the shift from analog to digital technology, and the idea that Sadako needs to understand modern technology and social media if she wants to continue cursing people. The summary for the English-language version of the manga tells us "No more climbing out of TVs, it's all about Youtube now!" (Amazon U.S. 2021). In the opening pages of the original Japanese manga, the older Sadako visits the younger, possibly "reborn" version of herself and is immediately shocked that the child has a smartphone. "Oh, that's normal now" (*imadoki futsū da yo*) says the child (Tsutsumi 2019, 6). She then refers to Sadako as an "ancient person" (*mukashi no hito*), which makes Sadako defensive ("I'm not an old woman! I climbed out of a well!" [Tsutsumi 2019, 6]). The child then explains to Sadako that everyone watches videos on their smartphones now. "If I climb out of a TV there won't be anyone there, and it'll be hard to curse anyone," Sadako realizes (Tsutsumi 2019, 10). Sadako then connects with "Fantastic Kazuma" to learn how to be a video content creator. A story framed within a comic book reveals how Sadako must "re-frame" *herself*, transitioning from the world of TVs and VCRs to the world of digital streaming.

Meanwhile, in the *Sadako* film, Kazuma is desperate to gain more followers on his channel and knows that "*shinrei* spot" videos are especially popular. He decides to film himself entering an old apartment complex where five people recently died in a fire. (It was in this apartment that the young girl who may be the reincarnation of Sadako lived until her mother decided to try to kill them both by setting the apartment on fire.) When his sister Mayu first encounters evidence of the video, Kazuma's friend tells her that it has been erased. But like the cursed Niconico video in *Sadako 3D*, it remains online even after being deleted—the curse is not so easily broken. (The ease of copying and sharing digital videos is also a plot point in *Sadako vs. Kayako*, where the cursed video is easily uploaded and shared with many people.) Even an absent thing has presence, and the empty space is the ideal place for a ghost to enter. Digital media itself has an element of spectrality beyond the presence of a malevolent spirit like Sadako.

Mayu eventually finds Kazuma's video on another site, and we cut back and forth between Mayu watching the video and the actual video itself. The cuts back to Mayu become fewer and further between, and at some point we seem to be merely watching a YouTube/Niconico video of a person exploring a burned-out building. Near the end of the video, Kazuma seems to see something terrifying and runs outside. When Mayu rewinds the video and pauses it right at a moment where the screen distorts and fills with static, there is an image of a skull embedded in the distortion. Slowing the video down again, she sees an image of a girl in white. Later, it seems that this strange black-and-white footage has embedded itself *within* other videos that Kazuma has uploaded online. An empty space, filled by a ghost. We see the image and the window of the computer screen reflected in Mayu's frightened eyes. We watch her, she watches the video, the video is reflected in her eyes. Kazuma's video is presented to the world through the very public venue of live streaming, but Mayu watches it in the privacy of her own home, on the small frame of her home computer, the image made all the more personal when we see it reflected in the much smaller space of her eyes (figure 4.2). Just as Sadako in this world moves easily between screens, devices, and platforms, the film reveals the permeability of the digital interface and the hazy distinction between public and private.

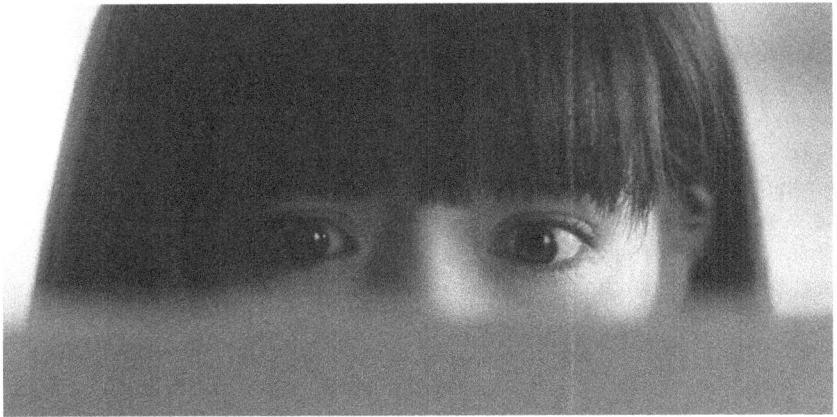

Figure 4.2 The computer screen is reflected in Mayu's eyes as she watches her brother's video in *Sadako* (Nakata Hideo 2019). *Source*: Screenshot taken by author.

The notion of gaps and the "nested *mise en abyme*" of videos-within-videos also plays out in the 2017 film *Rings*, a U.S.-made film that was very loosely based on Suzuki Kōji's novel *Spiral*.[6] Like *Sadako 3D* and *Sadako*, it also "upgrades" Sadako's curse, imagining a situation in which a university professor has created an experiment to prove the existence of the afterlife: he has taken Sadako's cursed video tape, converted it into a digital video, and devised an elaborate system of "tails" (students who watch the video and then immediately show it to someone else to avoid dying after seven days have passed). Now, as in *Sadako vs. Kayako*, *Sadako 3D*, and *Sadako*, sharing the video is simply a matter of copying and pasting a file. Here again, we see "gaps" in a recording, empty spaces in which ghosts or other malevolent presences can appear. The professor discovers that a newly copied digital version of the cursed video is larger than the original, and that an extra image has been inserted into it. "There's these weird gaps in the digital code," he says. "Glitches where we get these ghost images . . . We're talking one or two-frame still images, but there's more. There's video data condensed in the still frames." "A video within the video," another character responds (Gutiérrez 2017). Frames within frames, videos within videos. The cursed video's status as a new media object not only makes it easier to share and copy but also opens up the possibility of even more haunting in the gaps in its code, where new video data is condensed. The digital video is, in a sense, copying and mutating pieces of *itself* even as people in the film are actively copying and pasting it into different machines. Ultimately, the video "hacks" one character's e-mail account and sends itself to everyone in his contact list, who of course immediately view and share it, and Sadako's curse continues on.

Like *Sadako* and *Sadako 3D*, *Rings* makes use of multiple screens and frames, as well as the motif of staticky "snow" that appears in the original film and so many other Japanese "media horror" films. The film opens with Sadako invading an airplane through passengers' personal video monitors. Soon after, as the professor watches the video on a large TV screen seen through a rain-covered window, those windows momentarily become video screens, shifting to images of white static. At the end of the film, the main character, who has become a "vessel" for Sadako's rebirth, stares at herself in the mirror, which flickers and momentarily appears to be a staticky screen, before the woman wipes away the fog in the mirror to reveal Sadako's face staring back at her. Walls, windows, mirrors, and digital screens blur into each other and further blur the distinction between looking/being looked at.

The most memorable aspect of *Rings*, though, might be a publicity stunt that went viral in a manner similar to the cursed video within the narrative of the film. Viral marketing agency Thinkmodo set up TV screens and video cameras in an electronics store in White Plains, New York, with a young woman dressed as Sadako positioned behind a hole in the wall covered by a fake screen. As customers (who Thinkmodo claimed were actual customers and not actors) entered the store to look at TVs, the woman crawled out of the TV, causing the customers to shriek in horror (Matyszczyk 2017). The video of the stunt gained two hundred million views on Facebook, making it the most-viewed Facebook video ever at the time (Nudd 2017). It would go on to gain another ten million views on YouTube (as of April 2021). Thinkmodo cofounder James Percelay said of the stunt, "It's about taking things from a movie and putting them in a real-life context," he says. "There's no separation like there is in a movie trailer" (Nudd 2017). Windows and screens might often serve as a barrier between one world and another, but in this case the boundary is porous.

In the same way that the later *Ringu* films have moved Sadako between different platforms and screens, this stunt moves Sadako from the screen into the real world, playing with participants' sense of perspective (at one point when the actress playing Sadako is simply sitting, frozen, within the fake frame of a TV screen, one woman doesn't seem to realize that she is in fact not a video image). The fact that this publicity stunt was shared widely via platforms like Facebook and YouTube mirrors the reproduction and spread that happens in the *Rings* film, and in most entries in the *Ringu* franchise, illustrating the way that Sadako and so many horror images and characters break through literal and metaphorical boundaries, adding yet another layer to the *Ringu* franchise's long history of layering screens, frames, and perspectives.

In *Sadako 3D*, *Sadako*, and *Rings*, then, we can see the way that images and ideas are circulated not only via publicity stunts and the cross-platform promotion and development but also within the narratives of the films themselves, which see the entity of Sadako moving easily between Niconico broadcasts, YouTube videos, smartphones, computers, digital files, and the "gaps" in digital code that allow Sadako's cursed video to mutate and spread around the world. This "nested *mise en abyme*" extends as far back as J-horror's video production origins, and further into the realm of humorous manga frames and parody social media accounts. The materiality of the video cassette has transformed into the ephemerality of the digital video and digital file, one that spreads easily through copying and sharing, opens itself up to haunting through the empty spaces in its digital code, and can never truly be vanquished, given that its presence usually remains even after it has been deleted.

CONCLUSION

How do we tell scary stories, and how does the manner of their telling shape our perception of them? How do screens and new media devices/technologies further fracture our sense of reality and authenticity, creating new forms of fear and discomfort? As images, characters, and ideas from Japanese horror films are endlessly circulated and remediated, how does the significance of the films change? As I hope I have illustrated in this book's chapters, movement between screens and frames exists both inside and outside the narratives of Japanese horror films, informing not only the films' narratives but also the manner of their dissemination and consumption. A genre that has always dealt with the unease surrounding communication technology now presents an even more fractured reality through narratives that focus on the uncertainties created by digital media technology and devices. The occasional juxtaposition of old and new media technologies/devices in these films further illustrates how our manner of telling and sharing scary stories has changed over time, and the increasingly hazy distinctions between digital/physical and real/fictional. The young women in *Eiga: Toshimaen*, the idols in *Shirome*, the fictional visitors to Aokigahara, and the many iterations of Sadako circulate between screens, occasionally breaking through these porous barriers to further blur the boundaries between the "real" and digital worlds.

In the 2010s and beyond, Sadako's peak is far behind her—her images continue to circulate, but her ubiquity means that it is now difficult for her to inspire real terror. She is easily copied and pasted, edited, memed, reimagined for humorous videos or comic books, or used to sell bubble tea. But in the later *Ringu* sequels and remakes, she also illustrates the frightening power of a world made of screens, a world viewed through an endless series of virtual windows. Her (re)mediated self forces us to question the endlessly fractured reality in which we now live. The *Ringu* films and their many adjacent narratives are essentially stories of fragments scattered, collected, and re-shaped, pieces that tempt us toward the reveal of a cohesive whole, even if in the end the fractures remain.

NOTES

1. My thanks to Shaoling Ma and her student, Bryson Ng Pei Shen, for inspiring me to think about Galloway and the interface effect specifically in relation to the *Ringu* sequels.

2. Another horror film that effectively uses the footage-within-footage device is *Cloverfield*, which sees the characters using a video camera to record an alien invasion, not realizing that they are recording over video of a romantic day from the past. Within the film, footage of violence and terror occasionally cuts away to footage of two people having fun at Coney Island, reinforcing the sense of tragedy inherent in the film's main footage (which essentially ends with no survivors).

3. Julian Stringer notes that parody has been an aspect of the *Ringu* franchise since its early days, noting the 2003 release of a gay pornographic film, *The Hole*, which included the tagline "In seven days you will be gay, if you aren't already" (Stringer 2007, 299).

4. Named for the wide belt worn over a kimono, an *obi* is a small piece of paper that is often wrapped around the front and back flaps of a book or comic book sold in Japan, usually advertising another property sold by the same publisher.

5. Svensson and Hassoun (2016) note that the marketing campaign for *Sadako 3D 2* (dir. Hanabusa Tsutomu 2013) included a smartphone app that allowed users to receive phone calls and text messages connected to the film's narrative, further blurring the boundaries between personal screens and whatever screen one was using to watch the film itself.

6. *Sadako*, *Sadako 3D*, *Sadako 3D 2*, and *Rings* are variously described as being "loosely based" or "based on elements from" different Suzuki novels. However, beyond the presence of Sadako, the films bear little resemblance to the novels.

Conclusion
Living in Virtual Windows

I began this project in the mid-2010s by thinking about the role of old and new media objects and devices in Japanese horror films, how those objects and devices "frame" stories of ghosts and monsters, and how the circulation of certain narratives and images across "spatially and temporally fractured frames" contributes to an overall sense of fractured reality. I could not, of course, have imagined that for most of 2020 (and now, halfway through 2021), I would find myself very much confined within various types of screens, my communication with students, friends, family, coworkers, and colleagues generally limited to Zoom and other online platforms. The pandemic has caused massive loss of life, health, and livelihoods, and many people around the world have experienced intense trauma that will take a great deal of time to recover from. It has also, for many of us, fundamentally altered our relationships with screens, and by extension our relationship with media, communication, and personal relationships. Computers, smartphones, and tablets have become for many who were isolated for long periods of time, their only window onto the world.

Not surprisingly, horror filmmakers in Japan and around the world, limited in their activities by state of emergency declarations and overall safety concerns, found creative ways to make films during this time. In May 2020, director Ueda Shinichiro released a short "sequel" to his successful low-budget zombie film *One Cut of the Dead* (*Kamera wo tomeruna!*, 2017). Called *One Cut of the Dead: Mission: Remote* (*Kamera wo tomeru na! Rimōto daisakusen*), the roughly twenty-eight-minute film brought together the actors and crew of the original production to shoot an entirely "remote" TV special. Following COVID-19 quarantine restrictions, the actors each filmed themselves in their own homes, and then all of the footage was edited together to create the appearance of a film shot on a set as a group. Like *One Cut of the*

Dead, Remote had a zany creative energy and a feeling of wholesomeness that made it especially popular during the first state of emergency declared in Japan from April 7 to May 25, 2020, during which time the country effectively shut down. By the end of the film, though, the participants seem to be feeling genuine emotion—talking about how much they miss working on film sets together, or just doing everyday things like going to concerts and traveling. Tearfully, they promise each other, "*Mata, genba de*" ("See you soon, on set") (Ueda 2020).[1]

Horror film is a genre that typically relies on a great deal of bodily work from its performers—screaming, gasping, running, and fighting. Meaning is also derived from the community experience of gasping or screaming together in a theater, which was the main reason that Universal decided to delay the release of horror reboot *Candyman* until 2021, according to cowriter and director Nia DaCosta. On Twitter, DaCosta said that the film was meant to be seen in theaters, "not just for the spectacle but because the film is about community and stories—how they shape each other, how they shape us . . . It's about the collective experience of trauma and joy" (*Firstpost* 2020). In Japan, as in most other countries, movie theater attendance numbers have plummeted during the pandemic (*SankeiBiz* 2020), leading some producers and directors to take the unusual step of releasing their films via streaming services like Amazon instead of via theaters (or in addition to releasing the film a limited number of theaters).[2] But revenues for streaming services like Netflix have soared, given that so many people have few entertainment options other than watching movies and TV shows at home (Kafka 2020). Though Japan's vaccine rollout had picked up speed by mid-2021, it will likely be some time before "community" experiences of watching horror movies in a theater can happen again. Beyond safety concerns, it is still difficult to imagine what kinds of screens will dominate in a post-COVID-19 world—whether audiences will return to theaters, for example, or whether many will continue to primarily watch films, including horror films, at home on their personal computers, TVs, tablets, or smartphones.

Other "live" scare experiences in Japan, like haunted houses and roller coasters, have also been forced to find creative ways to deal with COVID-19 risks. The haunted house design company We Want to Scare You (*Kowagarasetai*) created a "drive-in" haunted house experience—participants sat in their cars in a parking garage while actors dressed as zombie-like monsters pawed at the car's windows. A local train company in Chōshi, Chiba Prefecture, got similarly creative. After seeing revenues plummet for its tourism-focused Chōshi Electric Railway, which runs through a very short section of the Chiba countryside, the company, which had previously held live "haunted train" events, crowdfunded a film called *Densha wo tomeru na!* (Don't stop the train!), a title clearly inspired by *One Cut of the Dead*. The film featured zombies and other supernatural creatures attacking riders on a train. Fuji-Q Highland and other amusement parks, on the other hand, sought to calm visitors' fears in unusual ways. In a web commercial that unwittingly reflected the frustration and anxiety many people were feeling after months of quarantine, confused messaging, and mass death and illness, two masked, suited executives from the Fuji-Q Highland amusement park were shown riding one of the park's roller coasters silently. They remained stoic throughout the ride, one of them conspicuously wearing a much-maligned "Abe-no-mask" (the too-small, cheaply made masks that the Abe government had sent to all Japanese households in April 2020). When the ride was over, text appeared on the screen: "Scream inside your heart" ("Zekkyō wa kokoro no naka de") (Fuji-Q Highland 2020). The responses on social media indicated that a lot of people were already doing so.

All of these examples reveal the many layers of mediation that exist between a frightening experience and the people who experience it, and the ways that this mediation has become even more complex during a pandemic that made in-person contact difficult for most. "Direct" horror experiences were forced to place both physical and digital barriers between participants: cars for a haunted house, a film experience for a train journey that would normally be live. For some, like the producers of *Candyman*, these barriers were unacceptable, and they opted to wait until their film could be experienced in groups in a theater. For others, the Zoom format presented yet another way to create horror experiences focused on screens and mediated reality.

After over a year of teaching, socializing, and attending conferences via Zoom, the technology has become mundane, but I can't help noticing its inherent spectrality during particularly long meetings or classes. People appear and disappear, their names or avatars popping in and out of the collection of black boxes depending on the strength of their Wi-Fi connections. Teaching to a gallery full of black screens can often feel like shouting into a void.[3] Poor Internet connections warp the sounds of people's voices, reminding me of the technologically mediated voices of ghosts that Konaka Chiaki and Takahashi Hiroshi found particularly frightening. Films like *Host* (dir. Robert Savage 2020), about a seance conducted over a Zoom gathering, clearly took advantage of these feelings of spectrality, as did the 2020 film *The Samejima Incident* (*Samejima jiken*, dir. Nagae Jirō), which begins with all of the main characters on a Zoom call that turns terrifying when one of the group's cameras begins broadcasting frightening video images. Beyond its potential for simple and interestingly framed horror narratives that don't require risky in-person contact, the simple act of using Zoom can also be an inherently ghostly experience.

In the midst of a global pandemic, I also find myself examining the more fundamental question of what function horror films serve in a world where a significantly larger number of people than usual are experiencing horrific things every day. I wonder about the role that new media will continue to play not only in horror narratives and the dissemination of horror images but also in propping up the more basic structures of the media industry. The technologies that Wendy Hui Kyong Chun described as both "wonderfully creepy" and "banal" have taken on new meaning during the pandemic. For many of us, Zoom and similar screen-based communication media are our only means of regularly communicating and connecting with other humans, a fact that engenders both gratitude and resentment. It's one thing for new media objects and new media devices to feel like a *component* of our lives, it's another for them to be a literal lifeline.[4] The horror now, it seems, comes not necessarily from the ubiquity of new media, but from the fact that it's all we have.

Interestingly, I have not found myself less inclined to seek out horror films for entertainment during the pandemic. I am happy to turn to stories of vengeful ghosts or haunted houses, which exist in a world where good and evil are defined much more clearly, and where the terror feels decidedly removed from the now-mundane terror of venturing out in public and feeling a surge of panic at the slightest sign of cold- or flu-like symptoms. For the most part, Japanese horror films have not caught up to the pandemic, and the images and narratives I have consumed during this time have been a reminder, ironically, of a *less* frightening time.

It remains to be seen when the Japanese film industry will return to any semblance of normalcy, or when we will be able to safely experience haunted houses, horror films in theaters, or displays of ghost-paintings in a temple or museum. It would seem that some aspects of this industry are already ready to get back to business as usual, though. As mentioned in the introduction, at Odaiba's Sega Joypolis, an indoor amusement park featuring VR attractions, video games, and "walk through" attractions based on Sega properties, a new "Sadako" walk-through attraction began in summer 2020. Called "*Sadako: Noroi furui no yakata*" ("Sadako: The Cursed Old Mansion"), the attraction yet again moves Sadako easily from one universe into another, this time imagining a "cursed fortune teller" who has attracted evil spirits into an old building that participants have to walk through. The website ad copy describes the fear experienced in the attraction as not "indirect" (*kansetsuteki*) but as a "fear that is close to a real experience" (*jitsutaiken to shite yori mijika ni kanjirareru kyōfu*) (Joypolis 2020). In May 2021, though, with much of Japan under yet another state of emergency that has forced many venues like Joypolis to temporarily close, it remains to be seen how much of a "real experience" visitors will be able to have in the near future.

Like so many other characters and images from Japanese horror films, then, Sadako has been able to move easily both around the world and within Japan, jumping between narratives, time periods, and platforms, existing as a bubble tea advertising gimmick, a flesh-and-blood scare in a haunted house attraction, a frightening image on a screen within a screen, an ironic Twitter user, and in a variety of promotional stunts. What makes the ad copy for this new attraction interesting is that Sadako has only rarely existed as a "direct" horror experience. Her existence has always been mediated, in multiple senses of the word. She first came to us through TV screens and a VHS cassette, then through the Internet and smart phones. She has always existed at a distance from us and, like the new media technologies and devices that we use constantly, became "banal" in the same moment that she was "wonderfully creepy." Now, in a time when, ironically, we are all keeping much more distance from our horror experiences, she is promoted as a direct, physical encounter.

Even before social media dominated our daily lives, Japanese horror films were fascinated by screens, by old media and new, by the inherent mix of appeal and anxiety that these technologies and their accompanying devices produced. Now we find ourselves in a world where communication technology is more widespread and influential than ever, and where the very structure of our social survival has become completely dependent on screens and various social media platforms, at least for the foreseeable future. It remains to be seen how much of this structure will linger after the worst of the pandemic has passed. But even if the Zoom-based horror films and zombie movies set on financially strapped trains are long gone, Japanese horror films' sense of "fractured reality," created via a multitude of spatially and temporally fractured frames, will likely continue.

NOTES

1. Aaron Gerow notes that several other Japanese directors and film production groups made "remote" films during the pandemic. These included the Stay Home Mini-Theater project, which made films in the "telework" style, and director Fukada Kōji, whose *The Yalta Conference Online* also utilized the Zoom format (Gerow 2020). In the United States, director Robert Savage created the film *Host*, the story of a Zoom-based séance, which takes place entirely in the context of a Zoom call and, in true found-footage fashion, sees actors playing characters with their same first names. David F. Sandberg, known for his short film *Lights Out* (later made into a feature-length film), created another three-minute short called *Shadowed*, which was filmed entirely in his home while he was in lockdown.

2. In a conversation filmed for the Tokyo International Film Festival's Asia Lounge series on the future of cinema and streaming, director Yukisada Isao said that during the pandemic he ultimately agreed to have his film *Theater: A Love Story* (*Gekijō* 2020) released simultaneously on Amazon and in a limited number of theaters, only because delaying release would mean tens of millions of yen more in

marketing costs. Yukisada made the point that he is a film director and wants to see his films in theaters, and other participants in the conversation also commented that films that are never released in theaters in Japan are often not eligible for awards, which can be important for a film's success (Tokyo International Film Festival 2021).

3. Zoom has made questions of public/private particularly fraught, especially when it comes to teaching and workplace communication. In Japan, many universities are reluctant to require students to turn on their cameras during Zoom classes, given that they may be connecting from a space with minimal privacy (and their computers or smartphones may lack the technology required to create virtual backgrounds).

4. I realize, of course, that for many people with disabilities, social media, and new media devices have always been a lifeline. The pandemic has simply made this the reality for a much larger number of people.

Bibliography

Akimoto, Akky. 2014. "Who Holds the Deeds to Gossip Bulletin Board 2channel?" *Japan Times*, March 20, 2014. https://www.japantimes.co.jp/life/2014/03/20/digital/who-holds-the-deeds-to-gossip-bulletin-board-2channel/.
Akkīna TV. 2021. YouTube channel. Accessed May 17, 2021. https://www.youtube.com/channel/UCbd6EoFvlkoVdcSImtbuouQ.
Allison, Anne. 2001. "Memoirs of the Orient." *Journal of Japanese Studies* 27, no. 2 (Summer): 381–398.
Amazon Japan. 1996–2020. *Kunekune* DVD Description. Accessed May 17, 2021. https://www.amazon.co.jp/-/en/dp/B0040X34QU.
Amazon U.S. 2021. Summary of *Sadako-san and Sadako-chan*. https://www.amazon.com/Sadako-san-Sadako-chan-Noriaki-Sugihara/dp/1648274188.
Ancuta, Katarzyna. 2007. "Ringu and the Vortex of Horror: Contemporary Japanese Horror and the Technology of Chaos." *Asian Journal of Literature, Culture and Society* 1, no. 1: 23–42.
Asai, Ryō. 1910. "Otogi bōko" [Hand Puppets]. In *Kinsei bungei sōso* [Collected Works of the Early Modern Period], vol. 3, edited by Hayakawa Junzaburō, 1–13. Tokyo: Takeki.
Ashby, Janet. 2002. "The Global Village: Small, but Not Always Beautiful." *Japan Times*, March 17, 2002. https://www.japantimes.co.jp/life/2002/03/17/lifestyle/the-global-village-small-but-not-always-beautiful/.
Attwood, Feona. 2007. "No Money Shot? Commerce, Pornography, and New Sex Taste Cultures." *Sexualities* 10, no. 4 (October): 441–456.
Azuma, Hiroki. 2009. *Otaku: Japan's Database Animals*. Translated by Jonathan E. Abel and Shion Kono. Minneapolis, MN: University of Minnesota Press.
Balmain, Colette. 2009. *Introduction to Japanese Horror Film*. Edinburgh: Edinburgh University Press.
Baudrillard, Jean. 2016 (1985). "The Masses: The Implosion of the Social in the Media." Translated by Marie Maclean. In *New Media, Old Media: A History and*

Theory Reader, edited by Wendy Hui Kyong Chun, Anna Watkins Fisher, and Thomas W. Keenan, 2nd edition, 525–522. New York: Routledge.

Bazin, Andre. 2005 (1967). "Painting and Cinema." In *What Is Cinema? Volume One*. Translated by Hugh Gray, 164–172. Berkeley, CA: University of California Press.

BBC News. 2013. "AKB48 Pop Star Shaves Head After Breaking Band Rules." February 1, 2013. https://www.bbc.com/news/world-asia-21299324.

Benedict, Ruth. 2005 (1946). *The Chrysanthemum and the Sword: Patterns of Japanese Culture*. New York: Houghton Mifflin.

Bereznak, Alyssa. 2019. "The 'Blair Witch' Extended Universe: How a Tiny Indie Film Became a Horror Sensation—And Invented Modern Movie Marketing." *The Ringer*, March 28, 2019. https://www.theringer.com/movies/2019/3/28/18280988/blair-witch-movie-marketing-1999.

Black, Daniel. 2012. "The Virtual Idol: Producing and Consuming Digital Femininity." In *Idols and Celebrity in Japanese Media Culture*, edited by Patrick W. Galbraith and Jason G. Karlin, 209–228. New York: Palgrave Macmillan.

Blake, Linnie, and Xavier Aldana Reyes. 2015. "Introduction: Horror in the Digital Age." In *Digital Horror: Haunted Technologies, Network Panic, and the Found Footage Phenomenon*, edited by Linnie Blake and Xavier Aldana Reyes, 13–31. London: Bloomsbury.

Bloomfield, Emma. 2018. "Thanaviewing, the Aokigahara Forest, and Orientalism: Rhetorical Separations Between the Self and the Other in *The Forest*." In *Virtual Dark Tourism: Ghost Roads*, edited by Kathryn N. McDaniel. New York: Palgrave Macmillan.

Box Office Mojo. 2021. "Japan Box Office For 2020." https://www.boxofficemojo.com/year/2020/?area=JP&grossesOption=calendarGrosses.

Braidotti, Rosi. 2011. "Allegro, ma non troppo. On Feminist Becomings." In *Intermedialities: Philosophy, Arts, Politics*, edited by Hugh J. Silverman, Henk Oosterling, and Ewa Plonowska-Ziarek, 99–111. Washington, DC: Lexington Books.

Broiler Chicken and Yoshie Mori. 2011. "Shinrei: Jukai de kokkuri-san" ["Spirits: Kokkuri-san in the Sea of Trees"]. YouTube Video, 7:56. March 25, 2011. https://www.youtube.com/watch?v=ooDfZS1aLvA&t=4s.

Brown, Steven T. 2018. *Japanese Horror and the Transnational Cinema of Sensations*. New York: Palgrave Macmillan.

Brunvand, Jan Harold. 2001. *Encyclopedia of Urban Legends*. New York: Norton.

———. 2003. *The Vanishing Hitchhiker: American Urban Legends and Their Meanings*. New York: Norton.

Choi, Stephanie. 2018. "Idol Singers' Intimate Labor in the Global Circulation of K-Pop." Paper presented at the *Association for Asian Studies Conference*, Washington, DC, March 22–25, 2018.

Chun, Wendy Hui Kyong. 2016a. "Introduction: Somebody Said New Media." In *New Media, Old Media: A History and Theory Reader*, edited by Wendy Hui Kyong Chun and Anna Watkins Fisher, 2nd edition, 1–16. New York: Routledge.

———. 2016b. *Updating to Remain the Same: Habitual New Media*. Cambridge, MA: MIT Press.

CinemaCafe.net. 2020. "Toshidensetsu wo eigaka 'Inunaki mura' TELASA nite senkō haishin kaishi! Bōtō 8-bu ga kōkai-chū" [From urban legend to movie: *Howling Village* will be available early on TELASA! First eight minutes available now!]. July 5, 2020. https://www.cinemacafe.net/article/2020/07/05/67901.html.

Debord, Guy. 1995 (1967). *The Society of the Spectacle*. Translated by Donald Nicholson-Smith. New York: Zone Books.

de Certeau, Michel. 1984. *The Practice of Everyday Life*. Translated by Steven Rendall. Berkeley, CA: University of California Press.

Derrida, Jacques. 1994. *Specters of Marx: The State of the Debt, the Work of Mourning, and the New International*. Translated by Peggy Kamuf. New York: Routledge.

Derrida, Jacques, and Bernard Stiegler. 2013. "Spectrographies." In *The Spectralities Reader: Ghosts and Haunting in Contemporary Cultural Theory*, edited by María del Pilar Blanco and Esther Pereen, 37–52. New York: Bloomsbury.

Dickey, Colin. 2016. *Ghostland: An American History in Haunted Places*. New York: Penguin.

DiMarco, Francesca. 2016. *Suicide in 20th-Century Japan*. New York: Routledge.

Dodds, Laurence. 2018. "The Story of Logan Paul Shows How the Modern Internet is Powered by Misery." *The Telegraph*, February 2, 2018. https://www.telegraph.co.uk/technology/2018/02/02/story-logan-paul-shows-modern-internet-powered-misery/.

Dumas, Raechel. 2018. *The Monstrous-Feminine in Contemporary Japanese Popular Culture*. New York: Palgrave Macmillan.

Dyer, Richard. 1979. *Stars*. London: British Film Institute.

Eiga: Toshimaen. 2020. "Sayonara yūenchi toshimaen kauntodaun jōei kettei!!" ["Goodbye Toshimaen amusement park countdown screening!"]. https://toshimaen-movie.tumblr.com/.

Endō, Hideo. 1967. *Fujisan: Rekishi to shinwa* [Mount Fuji: History and myth]. Tokyo: Terada shoten.

Enns, Anthony. 2010 "The Horror of Media: Technology and Spirituality in the *Ringu* Films." In *The Scary Screen: Media Anxiety in* The Ring," edited by Kristen Lacefield, 29–44. New York: Routledge.

Figal, Gerald. 2000. *Civilization and Monsters: Spirits of Modernity in Meiji Japan*. Durham, NC and London: Duke University Press.

Firstpost. 2020. "Universal moves *Candyman*'s release to 2020, director Nia DaCosta announces on Twitter." September 13, 2020. https://www.firstpost.com/entertainment/universal-moves-candymans-release-to-2021-director-nia-dacosta-announces-on-twitter-8812231.html.

Fischer's. 2016. "Fuji no jukai de *Pokemon Go* wo shitara chō rea pokemon ga arawareta" [When we played *Pokemon Go* in the Mount Fuji Sea of Trees, rare pokemon appeared]. YouTube Video, 8:18. July 24, 2016. https://www.youtube.com/watch?v=shjlJLJLX6A.

FISCO Ltd. 2017. "Company Research and Analysis Report: Kadokawa Dwango Corporation." July 3, 2017. https://www.fisco.co.jp/uploads/kadokawadwango20170703_e.pdf.

Foster, Michael Dylan. 2008. *Pandemonium and Parade: Japanese Monsters and the Culture of Yōkai*. Berkeley, CA: University of California Press.

Freedman, Alisa. 2009. "*Train Man* and the Gender Politics of Japanese 'Otaku' Culture: The Rise of New Media, Nerd Heroes and Consumer Communities." *Intersections: Gender and Sexuality in Asia and the Pacific* 20 (April). http://intersections.anu.edu.au/issue20/freedman.htm.

Friedberg, Anne. 2006. *The Virtual Window: From Alberti to Microsoft*. Cambridge, MA: MIT Press.

Fuji-Q Highland. 2020. "Magao charenji" [Straight face challenge]. YouTube video, 4:05. June 17, 2020. https://www.youtube.com/watch?v=PMm5QVZ6QeY.

Fuji-Yoshida kankō [Fuji-Yoshida sightseeing]. 2019. "Aokigahara tettei kaisetsu" [A thorough commentary on the Aokigahara Sea of Trees]. January 1, 2019. https://fujiyoshida-kanko.net/fujisan-history-aokigaharaforest/#dta2.

Fujita, Meiji, dir. 1991. *Nami no tō* [*Tower of waves*]. Tokyo: Fuji TV.

Galbraith, Patrick, and Jason G. Karlin. 2020. *AKB48*. New York: Bloomsbury Academic.

———. 2012. *Idols and Celebrity in Japanese Media Culture*. New York: Palgrave Macmillan.

Galloway, Alexander. 2012. *The Interface Effect*. Cambridge, MA: Polity Press.

———. 2013. "The Unworkable Interface." In *The Visual Culture Reader*, edited by Nicholas Mirzoeff, 3rd edition, 619–636. New York: Routledge.

Gerow, Aaron. 2002. "The Empty Return: Circularity and Repetition in Recent Japanese Horror Films." *Minikomi: Informationen des Akademischen Arbeitskreis Japan*, no. 64: 19–24.

———. 2020. "Japanese Film and the COVID Pandemic—Remotely in Space and Time." *Tangemania*, May 31, 2020. http://www.aarongerow.com/news/japanese-film-and-the-covid.html.

Gilhooly, Rob. 2011. "Inside Japan's 'Suicide Forest.'" *Japan Times*, June 26, 2011. https://www.japantimes.co.jp/life/2011/06/26/general/inside-japans-suicide-forest/#.WqXaGIKYMdU.

Goldberg, Ruth. 2004. "Demons in the Family: Tracking the Japanese 'Uncanny Mother Film' from *A Page of Madness* to *Ringu*." In *Planks of Reason: Essays on the Horror Film*, edited by Barry Keith Grant and Christopher Sharrett, revised edition, 370–385. Lanham, MD: Scarecrow Press.

Goldstein-Gidoni, Ofra. 2001. "The Making and Marking of the 'Japanese' and the 'Western' in Japanese Contemporary Material Culture." *Journal of Material Culture* 6, no. 1: 67–90.

Goyer, David S. 2016. *The Forest*. iTunes special features interview. New York: Gramercy Pictures. Streaming purchase.

Gray, Jonathan. 2010. *Show Sold Separately: Promos, Spoilers, and Other Media Paratexts*. New York: New York University Press.

Gray, Kyrie. 2020. "Be Careful When You Play the Elevator Game." *Medium*, October 22, 2020. https://medium.com/here-there-be-monsters/be-careful-when-you-play-the-elevator-game-bf3530f05882.

Gunning, Tom. 2013. "To Scan a Ghost: The Ontology of Mediated Vision." In *The Spectralities Reader: Ghosts and Haunting in Contemporary Cultural Theory*, edited by María del Pilar Blanco and Esther Peeren, 207–244. New York: Bloomsbury.

Gutiérrez, F. Javier, dir. 2017. *Rings*. Los Angeles: Vertigo Entertainment.

Hadfield, James. 2019. "Japan's Decade of Closed Country Cinema." *Japan Times*, November 14, 2019. https://www.japantimes.co.jp/culture/2019/11/14/films/japans-decade-closed-country-cinema/.

Hanabusa, Tsutomu, dir. 2012. *Sadako 3D*. Tokyo: Kadokawa. Netflix Japan.

Heidegger, Martin. 1977 (1954). "The Question Concerning Technology." In *The Question Concerning Technology and Other Essays*, translated by William Lovitt, 3–35. New York: Garland Publishing.

Hekitora Hausu. 2017. "Kurisumasu no jukai de jisatsu-sha wo tomeru" [Stopping suicides at Christmas in the Sea of Trees]. 2017. YouTube Video, 6:40. January 7, 2017. https://www.youtube.com/watch?v=irfBTTnKZvI.

Heller-Nicholas, Alexandra. 2014. *Found Footage Horror Films: Fear and the Appearance of Reality*. Jefferson: McFarland.

Iles, Timothy. 2005. "The Problem of Identity in Contemporary Japanese Horror Films." *Electronic Journal of Contemporary Japanese Studies* 5, no. 2. http://www.japanesestudies.org.uk/discussionpapers/2005/Iles2.html.

Imdb.com. 2021. "The Forest." https://www.imdb.com/title/tt3387542/.

Inaho Radio. 2019. "Shiraishi Kōji kantoku ni intabyū!" [Interview with director Shiraishi Kōji!]. October 14, 2019. https://inahoradio.com/2019/10/13/shiraishikouji-4/.

Ishii, Teruyoshi, dir. 1988. *Jaganrei* [Psychic Vision]. Tokyo: Pony Canyon. Amazon Japan Prime Video.

Itō, Ryūhei. 2016. *Netto roa: Webbu jidai no'hanashi' no densho* [Net lore: Stories of folklore in the internet age]. Tokyo: Seikyusha.

———. 2014. "Zoku 'Kunekune' kō: netto roa to denshō-tai" [A further consideration of 'Kunekune': Net lore and folklore]. Research discussion group #21. Tokyo: Iwata Shoin.

Ivy, Marilyn. 1995. *Discourses of the Vanishing: Modernity, Phantasm, Japan*. Chicago, IL: Chicago University Press.

Jenkins, Henry. 2006. *Convergence Culture: Where Old and New Media Collide*. New York: NYU Press.

Joypolis. 2020. "Kitto kuru… Sadako, noroi uranai no yakata" ["She's coming… Sadako, Curse of the Psychic Manor"]. https://tokyo-joypolis.com/language/english/attraction/sadako.html.

Kafka, Peter. 2020. "The pandemic has been great for Netflix." *Vox*, July 16, 2020. https://www.vox.com/recode/2020/7/16/21327451/netflix-covid-earnings-subscribers-q2.

Kaidan News-a. "*Kinkisaki / Pandora* no arasuji / kansō no matome / 2ch no kowai hanashi" [Plot of *Kinkisaki / Pandora* / Summary / 2ch Scary stories]. https://kyofu.takeshobo.co.jp/news/2ch-horror/167/.

Kaidan News-b. "Mokugeki shita mono wa ki ga kurū? Nazo no yōkai 'kunekune' no arasuji / kansō matome / 2 ch no kowai hanashi" ["Do those who witness it go crazy? Synopsis and impressions of the 2channel scary story of the mysterious 'kunekune' monster"]. https://kyofu.takeshobo.co.jp/news/column/2ch-horror/384/.

Kaidan News-c. "Kotoribako." https://kyofu.takeshobo.co.jp/news/column/2ch-horror/63/.

Katayama, Lisa. 2008. "Meet Hiroyuki Nishimura, the Bad Boy of the Japanese Internet." *Wired*, May 19, 2008. https://www.wired.com/2008/05/mf-hiroyuki/.

Keefe, Alexa. 2017. "An Ethereal Forest Where the Japanese Commit Suicide." *National Geographic*, February 23, 3017. https://www.nationalgeographic.com/photography/proof/2017/02/aokigahara-jukai-suicide-forest/.

Kidwell, Emma. 2018. "Logan Paul (and the internet) need to stop treating Japan as clickbait." *The Verge*, January 11, 2018. https://www.theverge.com/2018/1/11/16875188/logan-paul-aokigahara-suicide-forest-japan.

Kikkawa, Hisatake, dir. 2010. *Kunekune*. Tokyo: Video Maker. Amazon Japan Prime Video.

Kinoshita, Chika. 2009. "The Mummy Complex: Kurosawa Kiyoshi's *Loft* and J-horror." In *Horror to the Extreme: Changing Boundaries in Asian Cinema*, edited by Jinhee Choi and Mitsuyo Wada-Marciano, 103–122. Hong Kong: Hong Kong University Press.

Kitada, Akihiro. 2012. "Japan's Cynical Nationalism." Translated by Elissa Sato and Itō Mizuko. In *Fandom Unbound: Otaku Culture in a Connected World*, edited by Mizuko Ito, Daisuke Okabe, and Izumi Tsuji, 68–84. New Haven, CT: Yale University Press.

Kitajima, Yoshimasa. 2012. "Why Make E-moe-tional Attachments to Fictional Characters?: The Cultural Sociology of the Postmodern." Translated by Leonie R. Stickland. In *Pop Culture and the Everyday in Japan: Sociological Perspectives*, edited by Minamida Katsuya and Tsuji Izumi, 149–170. Melbourne, Australia: Trans Pacific Press.

Kittler, Friedrich. 1999 (1986). *Gramophone, Film, Typewriter*. Translated by Geoffrey Winthrop-Young and Michael Wutz. Palo Alto: Stanford University Press.

Koma, Natsumi. 2019. *Shūmatsu no Sadako-san* [Sadako at the end of the world]. Tokyo: Kadokawa.

Komatsu, Kazuhiko. 2017. *An Introduction to Yōkai Culture: Monsters, Ghosts, and Outsiders in Japanese History*. First edition. Translated by Hiroko Yoda and Matt Alt. Tokyo: Japan Publishing Industry Foundation for Culture.

Konaka, Chiaki. 2003. *Horā eiga no miryoku: fandamentaru horā seigen* [The fascination of horror films: A manifesto of fundamental horror]. Tokyo: Iwanami Shoten, 2003.

Kurosawa, Kiyoshi. 2001a. *Eiga wa osoroshii* [Movies are scary]. Tokyo: Seidosha.

———, dir. 2001b. *Kairo* [Pulse]. Tokyo: Toho. DVD.

Lacefield, Kristen. 2010. "Introduction." In *The Scary Screen: Media Anxiety in* The Ring, edited by Kristen Lacefield, 1-28. New York: Ashgate.

Laird, Colleen. 2021. "UBC Conversations with J Horror Scholars: Interview with Prof. Chika Kinoshita on Kurosawa Kiyoshi's 'Loft.'" March 9, 2021. YouTube video, 1:18:38. https://www.youtube.com/watch?v=LMoH3skWAX8.

Larsen, Miranda. 2019. "Cult Conversations: Desktop Horror and Captive Cinema." *Henry Jenkins: Confessions of an Aca-Fan* (blog). February 12, 2019. http://henryjenkins.org/blog/2019/2/10/cult-conversations-desktop-horror-and-captive-cinema-by-miranda-ruth-larsen.

Livedoor News. 2016. "'Pokemon Go' ga jisatsu wo fusegu? Fan dai yorokobi 'Tsugi wa Fuji no jukai da'" ["Is *Pokemon Go* preventing suicides? Fans are really happy: 'Next, Mt. Fuji's Sea of Trees'"]. Sepember 7, 2016. https://news.livedoor.com/article/detail/11988322/.

Lukacs, Gabriella. 2010. *Scripted Affects, Branded Selves: Television, Subjectivity, and Capitalism in 1990s Japan*. Durham, NC: Duke University Press.

Maekawa, Osamu. 2015. "*Ringu* no futatsu no imi: *Ringu* no iconolojī to iconomī (Ringing *Ringu*: From iconology to iconomy)." *Bigaku geijutsugaku ronshuu* (Journal of aesthetics and arts) 11: 6–20. Departmental bulletin paper. http://www.lib.kobe-u.ac.jp/repository/81008810.pdf.

Mainichi Shinbun. 2017. "Fuji ga hagukunda gensei-rin, kankō meisho e ninkiji wari" ["Mount Fuji nurtured a primeval forest that is becoming a popular sightseeing spot."]. December 26, 2017. https://mainichi.jp/articles/20171226/k00/00e/040/265000c.

———. 2021. "Jisatsu tōkei sokuhō-chi, Yamanashi ga jinkō-hi de wāsuto haikei ni 'hai risuku-chi' to ken bunseki" ["Based on preliminary statistics, Yamanashi Prefecture suicide rate is highest by population: "high risk" background and prefectural analysis"]. January 26, 2021. https://mainichi.jp/articles/20210126/k00/00m/040/208000c.

———. 2020. "Toshimaen dankai-teki heien e atochi ni 23-nen haripota shisetsu saigai hinan basho mo" ["Toshimaen to close, area will become a Harry Potter theme park and disaster evacuation site by 2023"]. https://mainichi.jp/articles/20200203/k00/00m/040/063000c.

Makuch Leonie. 2014. "Ekusutorīmu chikubi sumō in aokigahara jukai" [Extreme nipple sumo in the Aokigahara Sea of Trees]. 2014. YouTube Video, 4:39. June 8, 2014. https://www.youtube.com/watch?v=rIi7Q0vyNzc.

Manovich, Lev. 2001. *The Language of New Media*. Cambridge, MA: MIT Press.

Marx, W. David. 2012. "The *Jimusho* System: Understanding the Production Logic of the Japanese Entertainment Industry." In *Idols and Celebrity in Japanese Media Culture*, edited by Patrick Galbraith and Jason G. Karlin, 35–55. New York: Palgrave Macmillan.

Matomedia. 2013. "Kunekune mitakoto aru yatsu iru?" [Anyone here seen *Kunekune*?]. September 21, 2013. http://totalmatomedia.blog.fc2.com/blog-entry-1270.html.

Matsumoto, Seichō. 1960. *Nami no tō* [Tower of waves]. Tokyo: Bungei Shunjū.

Matsuzaki, Takeo. 2020. "Nakata Hideo: Kantoku intabyū" [Nakata Hideo: Director interview]. *Kinema Junpo* 1847 (September 1, 2020): 14–17.

Matyszczyk, Chris. 2017. "Horror film stunt frightens TV shoppers, gets 10M Facebook views." *cnet*, January 23, 2017. https://www.cnet.com/news/horror-movie-rings-publicity-stunt-electronic-store-real-shoppers/.

McRoy, Jay. 2005. "Introduction." In *Japanese Horror Cinema*, edited by Jay McRoy, 1–11. Honolulu, HI: University of Hawai'i Press.

Mes, Tom, and Jasper Sharp. 2005. *The Midnight Eye Guide to New Japanese Film*. Berkeley, CA: Stone Bridge Press.

Minear, Richard. 1980. "Review: Orientalism and the Study of Japan." *The Journal of Asian Studies* 39, no. 3: 507–517.

Momoiro Clover Z Live History. 2018. Momoiro Clover Z official website. Accessed May 17, 2021. https://www.momoclo.net/mcz_history/.

Momoiro Clover Z Wiki. 2014. http://momoirocloverz.wikia.com/wiki/Momoiro_Clover_Z.

Morioka, Heinz, and Miyoko Sasaki. 1990. *Rakugo: The Popular Narrative Art of Japan*. Cambridge, MA: Harvard University Press.

Morley, David, and Kevin Robins. 1995. *Spaces of Identity: Global Media, Electronic Landscapes, and Cultural Boundaries*. New York: Routledge.

Motohashi, Yutaka. 2011. "Suicide in Japan." *The Lancet* 379, no. 9823: 1282–1283.

Movie Collection. 2021. "Hontō no 'aokigahara jukai' to wa…? Eiga *Jukai Mura* × Yamanashi ken korabo dōga" [What is the real 'Aokigahara Sea of Trees'? A video collaboration between Yamanashi prefecture and the film *Suicide Forest Village*]. YouTube video, 0:30. February 3, 2021. https://www.youtube.com/watch?v=3D0EuUC-WnQ.

———. 2010. "*Shirome* Momoiro Clover Interview." August 12, 2010. http://www.moviecollection.jp/interview/detail.html?p=605.

MPAJ (Motion Picture Producers Association of Japan, Inc). 2021. http://www.eiren.org/toukei/data.html.

Myrick, Daniel, and Eduardo Sánchez, dir. 1999. *The Blair Witch Project*. Orlando, FL: Haxan Films. iTunes.

Nagae, Jirō, dir. 2010. *Webbukamera tsūwa* [Webcam Call]. In *2channeru no noroi, vol. 1* [2channel Curse, Volume One]. Tokyo: Jolly Roger. Amazon Japan Prime Video.

Nakamura, Noboru, dir. 1960. *Nami no tō* [Tower of waves]. Tokyo: Shochiku. Amazon Japan Prime Video.

Nakata, Hideo, dir. 1996. *Joyūrei* [Don't Look Up]. Tokyo: Bandai Visual. DVD.

———, dir. 1998. *Ringu* [The Ring]. Tokyo: Pony Canyon. DVD.

———. 2019. *Sadako*. Tokyo: Kadokawa. Netflix Japan.

Nakayama, Yuto. 2016. "Netto roa ni miru gendai no kaiiteki sekaikan to keikan imēji kenkyū" ["Looking at the modern 'mysterious world' through research on geographical images of 'net lore'"]. Graduation thesis, Takahiro Sasaki seminar, Kyoto University of Advanced Science. https://lab.kuas.ac.jp/~jinbungakkai/pdf/2016/h2016_02.pdf.

Napier, Susan. 2011. "Where Have All the Salarymen Gone? Masochism, and Technomobility in *Densha Otoko*." In *Recreating Japanese* Men, edited by Sabine Frühstück and Anne Walthall, 154–176. Berkeley, CA: University of California Press.

Negroponte, Nicholas. 1995. *Being Digital*. New York: Alfred A. Knopf.

Nelson, Lindsay. 2012. "Embracing the Demon: The Monstrous Child in Japanese Literature and Cinema, 1946-2009." PhD dissertation, University of Southern California.

Nems, Alexandra. 2015. "A forest of death at the base of Mount Fuji." *Stars and Stripes Japan*, January 16, 2015. https://japan.stripes.com/community-news/forest-death-base-mount-fuji-1547824653.

Nifty News. 2020. "*Inunaki Mura* de tettō kara tobiorita 'akkīna' dai 2-dan 'jukaimura' ni mo shutsuen yūchūbu chan'neru kaisetsu" ["'Akkīna,' who jumped from a steel tower in *Howling Village* and appears in the second film, *Suicide Forest Village*, has created a YouTube channel"]. October 14, 2020. https://news.nifty.com/article/entame/movie/12119-826057/.

Nihon Keizai Shinbun. 2012. "Yamanashi-ken, Aokigahara jukai de jisatsu daizai no roke okotawari" ["Yamanashi prefecture refuses to allow location shooting in the Aokigahara Sea of Trees for content related to suicide"]. November 24, 2012. https://r.nikkei.com/article/DGXNASDG2301E_U2A121C1CC0000?s=6.

Nudd, Tim. 2017. "The Story Behind the Pants-Soiling 'Rings' Prank That Has 200 Million Views in 24 Hours." *Adweek*, January 24, 2017. https://www.adweek.com/creativity/story-behind-pants-soiling-rings-prank-has-200-million-views-24-hours-175720/.

Oricon News. 2020. "'Toshimaen' karūseru erudorado, saishū unten o shūryō kaitai shi mentenansu e" ["Carousel El Dorado runs for the last time, will be disassembled for maintenance"]. August 31, 2020. https://www.oricon.co.jp/news/2170643/full/.

Ōsawa, Shinichi. 2010. "Paris." YouTube video, 4:47. November 15, 2010. https://www.youtube.com/watch?v=XuUq-JYKusg.

Ōshima, Kiyoaki. 2010. *J horā no yūrei kenkyū* [J-horror ghost research]. Tokyo: Akiyama shoten.

Ōtake, Tomoko. 2017. "Suicides down, but Japan still second highest among major industrialized nations, report says." *Japan Times*, May 30, 2017. https://www.japantimes.co.jp/news/2017/05/30/national/social-issues/preventive-efforts-seen-helping-2016-saw-another-decline-suicides-japan-21897/.

Ōtsuka, Eiji. 2010. "World and Variation: The Reproduction and Consumption of Narrative." Translated by Marc Steinberg. In *Mechademia 5: Fanthropologies*, edited by Frenchy Lunning, 99–116. Minneapolis, MN: University of Minnesota Press.

Peli, Oren, dir. 2007. *Paranormal Activity*. Los Angeles, CA: Blumhouse Productions. iTunes.

Pereira, Alyssa. 2016. "Japanese taxi drivers claim 'ghost passengers' hail cabs at site of 2011 tsunami." *SFGate*, February 4, 2016. https://www.sfgate.com/news/article/Japanese-taxi-drivers-claim-ghost-passengers-6806980.php.

Pinedo, Isabel Christina. 1997. *Recreational Terror: Women and the Pleasures of Horror Film Viewing*. Albany, NY: State University of New York Press.

PopSugar Entertainment. 2016. "Japan's Suicide Forest Is Even Scarier Than It Sounds." YouTube video, 2:09. April 24, 2016. https://www.youtube.com/watch?v=CHSP262dkDw.

Powdermaker, Hortense. 2013 (1950). *Hollywood, the Dream Factory: An Anthropologist Looks at the Movie-Makers*. Mansfield Center, CT: Martino Fine Books.

Puchko, Kristy. 2016. "15 Eerie Things About Japan's Suicide Forest." *Mental Floss*, January 8, 2016. https://www.mentalfloss.com/article/73288/15-eerie-things-about-japans-suicide-forest.

RBB Today. 2013. "Ano AKB 48 'chō ōgata shinjin' Eguchi Aimi ga sotsugyō!? Kōshiki saito-jō kara namae ga kie fan sōzen" [That 'amazing AKB48 rookie' Eguchi Aimi graduated!? Fans upset after her name disappears from website]. May 8, 2013. http://www.rbbtoday.com/article/2013/05/08/107583.html.

Rear, Jack. 2018. "What is the Aokigahara forest in Japan and can you visit it?" *Verdict*, January 2, 2018. https://www.verdict.co.uk/aokigahara-forest-japan-can-visit/.

Reider, Noriko T. 2000. "The Appeal of 'Kaidan,' Tales of the Strange." *Asian Folklore Studies* 59, no. 2: 265–283.

Rich, Motoko. 2018. "Long Before Video, Japanese Fought Suicide in the 'Sea of Trees.'" *New York Times*, January 5, 2018. https://www.nytimes.com/2018/01/05/world/asia/suicide-forest-japan-logan-paul.html.

Robertson, Adi. 2015. "The man whose site inspired 4chan is now running 4chan." *Verge*, September 21, 2015. https://www.theverge.com/2015/9/21/9364499/2channel-hiroyuki-nishimura-buys-4chan.

Rojas, Carlos. 2014. "Viral Contagion in the *Ringu* Intertext," In *The Oxford Handbook of Japanese Cinema*, edited by Daisuke Miyao, 416–437. Oxford: Oxford University Press.

Romano, Aja. 2018. "Logan Paul and the Toxic YouTube Prank Culture that Created Him, Explained." *Vox*, January 3, 2018. https://www.vox.com/2018/1/3/16841160/logan-paul-aokigahara-suicide-controversy.

Roy, Sandip. 2010. "The New Colonialism of *Eat, Pray, Love*." *Salon*, August 14, 2010. https://www.salon.com/2010/08/14/i_me_myself/.

Rucka, Nicholas. 2005. "The Death of J-Horror?" *Midnight Eye*, December 22, 2005. http://www.midnighteye.com/features/the-death-of-j-horror/.

Said, Edward. 1978. *Orientalism*. 25th anniversary edition. New York: Vintage Books.

Sakai, Naoki. 1989. "Modernity and Its Critique: The Problem of Universalism and Particularism." In *Postmodernism and Japan*, edited by Masao Miyoshi and Harry D. Harootunian, 93–122. Durham, NC and London: Duke University Press.

Sakamoto, Rumi. 2011. "'Koreans, Go Home!' Internet Nationalism in Contemporary Japan as Digitally Mediated Subculture." *The Asia-Pacific Journal* 9, no. 10: 2. https://apjjf.org/2011/9/10/Rumi-SAKAMOTO/3497/article.html.

Sankei News. 2020. "Kyōfu eiga gyakute ni jukai PR Yamanashi ken `jisatsu jochō' kara itten, daki-tsuki senpō" [Yamanashi prefecture once saw scary movies made in Aokigahara as 'promoting suicide,' but their new strategy is to embrace the forest's image]. November 30, 2020. https://www.sankei.com/premium/news/201130/prm2011300003-n1.html.

SankeiBiz. 2020. "Kyaku ashi wa nibui ga 8-wari chō 'anshin dekita' korona jidai no eigakan wa igai to anzen?" [Although attendance has dropped more than 80%, movie theaters in the age of coronavirus are surprisingly safe: "I was relieved"].

August 17, 2020. https://www.sankeibiz.jp/business/news/200817/bsd20081707 02001-n1.htm.
Sayad, Cecilia. 2016. "Found-Footage Horror and the Frame's Undoing." *Cinema Journal* 55, no. 2: 43–66.
Scherer, Elisabeth. 2016 "Well-Traveled Female Avengers: The Transnational Potential of Japanese Ghosts." In *Ghost Movies in Southeast Asia and Beyond*, edited by Peter J. Bräunlein and Andrea Lauser, 61–82. Leiden and Boston: Brill.
Sconce, Jeffrey. 2000. *Haunted Media: Electronic Presence from Telegraphy to Television.* Durham, NC: Duke University Press.
———. 2010. "Haunted Networks." In *The Scary Screen: Media Anxiety in* The Ring, edited by Kristen Lacefield, 215–221. New York: Ashgate.
Sharrett, Christopher. 2005. "Preface: Japanese Horror Cinema." In *Japanese Horror Cinema*, edited by Jay McRoy, xi–xiv. Honolulu, HI: University of Hawai'i Press.
Shimizu, Takashi, dir. 2021. *Jukai mura* [Suicide forest village]. Tokyo: Tōei.
Shinjō, Taku, dir. 2012. *Aokigahara.* Tokyo: Taku Shinjō Production. DVD.
Shiraishi, Kōji, dir. 2016. *Feiku dokyumentarī no kyōkasho* [Fake documentary textbook]. Tokyo: Seibundo.
———. 2010a. *Bachiatari bōryoku ningen* [Cursed violent people]. Tokyo: Creative Axa. Amazon Japan Prime Video.
———. 2009. *Okaruto* [Occult]. Tokyo: Creative Axa. Amazon Japan Prime Video.
———. 2010b. *Shirome.* Tokyo: Stardust Promotions. DVD.
SPARROW AIM-7P. 2021. "2021/05/07 Fri Total post count." http://stat.5ch.net/SPARROW/20210507/.
Steinberg, Marc. 2019. *The Platform Economy: How Japan Transformed the Consumer Internet.* Minneapolis, MN: University of Minnesota Press.
Steinberg, Marc, and Alexander Zahlten. 2017. "Introduction." In *Media Theory in Japan*, edited by Marc Steinberg and Alexander Zahlten, 14–54. Durham, NC and London: Duke University Press.
Stringer, Julian. 2007. "The Original and the Copy: Nakata Hideo's *Ring* (1998)." In *Japanese Cinema: Texts and Contexts*, edited by Alastair Philips and Julian Stringer, 296–307. Oxford: Routledge.
Strusiewicz, Cezary Jan. 2009. "The 6 Creepiest Places on Earth." *Cracked.com*, October 27, 2009. https://www.cracked.com/article_181_the-6-creepiest-places-earth.html.
Studio 360. 2009. "Suicide Forest." January 30, 2009. https://www.wnycstudios.org/podcasts/studio/segments/107979-suicide-forest.
Suzuki, Krys. 2019. "Drowning in a Sea of Trees: Understanding Aokigahara, Japan's 'Suicide Forest.'" *Unseen Japan*, March 21, 2019. https://unseenjapan.com/aokigahara-forest/.
Svensson, Alexander, and Dan Hassoun. 2016. "'Scream into Your Phone': Second Screen Horror and Controlled Interactivity." *Participations: Journal of Audience and Reception Studies* 13, no. 1: 170–192.

Taito City Culture Guide Archives. 2019. "Hanayashiki ni asobu" [Have fun at Hanayashiki]. https://www.culture.city.taito.lg.jp/bunkatanbou/city/hanayashiki/japanese/page_01.html.

Takahashi, Hiroshi. 2004. *Eiga no ma* [The magic of cinema]. Tokyo: Seidosha.

Takahashi, Hiroshi, dir. 2019. *Eiga: Toshimaen* [Toshimaen: The Movie]. Tokyo: Tōei. Netflix Japan.

Takahashi, Yoshimoto. 1988. "Suicide and Amnesia in Mt. Fuji's Black Forest." *Suicide and Life-Threatening Behavior* 18, no. 2: 164–175.

tokoroda. 2014. "*Shirome*: Eiga kokuchi tōku, Momoiro Clover" [*Shirome*: Movie announcement discussion, Momoiro Clover"]. YouTube video, 8:11. February 2, 2014. https://www.youtube.com/watch?v=vpAI1aQvovM.

Tōkō-sū tōkei@ 2ch keijiban [Post statistics@2ch bulletin board]. 2021. "Sōtōkōsū" ["Total number of posts"]. https://sweet.2ch.sc/posts.html.

Tokyo DailyPhoto. 2012. "Suicide Forest in Japan - Aokigahara, Also Known as the Sea of Trees." YouTube video, 26:41. July 25, 2012. https://www.youtube.com/watch?v=9Kkv89OhJEI.

Tokyo International Film Festival. 2021. "Asia Lounge Special Session: The Future of Cinema and Streaming." YouTube Video, 1:40:58. January 26, 2021. https://www.youtube.com/watch?v=rIJc_O95cV0&t=1147s.

Tsutsumi, Aya. 2019. *Sadako-san to Sadako-chan* [Sadako-san and Sadako-chan]. Tokyo: Kadokawa.

Ueda, Shinichiro. 2020. *Kamera wo tomeru na! Rimōto daisakusen* [One Cut of the Dead: Mission: Remote]. YouTube video, 26:15. May 15, 2020. https://www.youtube.com/watch?v=5QGi6Y6NZLI&t=1383s.

Vice. 2012. "Suicide Forest in Japan (Full Documentary." 21:08. YouTube video, May 10, 2012. https://www.youtube.com/watch?v=4FDSdg09df8.

Wada-Marciano, Mitsuyo. 2012. *Japanese Cinema in the Digital Age*. Honolulu, HI: University of Hawai'i Press.

Wee, Valerie. 2014. *Japanese Horror Films and Their American Remakes*. New York: Routledge.

White, Eric. 2005. "Case Study: Nakata Hideo's *Ringu* and *Ringu 2*." In *Nightmare Japan*, edited by Jay McRoy, 38–47. Boston, MA: Rodopi.

Williams, Linda. 1991. "Film Bodies: Gender, Genre, and Excess." *Film Quarterly* 4, no. 4: 2–13.

Yahoo! Japan. 2011. "Momoiro Clover no eiga, *Shirome* wo mita kata ni…" ["To people who have seen Momoiro Clover's movie *Shirome*…"]. September 2, 2011. http://detail.chiebukuro.yahoo.co.jp/qa/question_detail/q1370344588.

———. 2021. "Shōgakusei danshi ga naritai shokugyō, 3-i 'sakkā senshu', 2-i 'YouTuber', 1-i wa?" ["What do elementary school boys want to be when they grow up? Number three is soccer player, number two is YouTuber: what's number one?"]. March 17, 2021. https://news.yahoo.co.jp/articles/f99074ff32bd98b517258 73e5c72473caf125854.

Yamanashi Prefecture. 2019. "Fuji tōbu hokenjo ni okeru jisatsu bōshi no torikumi ni tsuite" ["On suicide prevention efforts at the Fuji / eastern health center"].

Yamanashi Prefecture website, December 10, 2019. https://www.pref.yamanashi.jp/ft-hokenf/suicide-guideline1.html.

Yomota, Inuhiko. 2019. *What Is Japanese Cinema? A History*. Translated by Philip Kaffen. New York: Columbia University Press.

Yoshino, Kosaku. 1992. *Cultural Nationalism in Japan: A Sociological Inquiry*. New York: Routledge.

Yu, Sabrina Qiong. 2017. "Performing Stardom: Star Studies in Transformation and Expansion." In *Revisiting Star Studies: Cultures, Themes and Methods*, edited by Sabrina Qiong Yu and Guy Austin, 1–22. Cambridge, MA: Cambridge University Press.

Zada, Jason, dir. 2016a. *The Forest*. New York: Gramercy Pictures. iTunes.

———. 2016b. *The Forest*. iTunes special features interview. New York: Gramercy Pictures. iTunes.

Zahlten, Alexander. 2017. *The End of Japanese Cinema: Industrial Genres, National Times, and Media Ecologies*. Durham, NC and London: Duke University Press.

Index

AKB48, 12, 51–55, 61, 69
advertising trucks, 91, 103
Allison, Anne, 82
analog media, 26, 96, 105; celluloid, 18, 22, 50, 93–95, 105; film negatives, 4, 18; paper photographs, 18, 41, 45, 95; video cassettes, 3, 7, 10, 18–19, 22, 40, 44, 92, 96, 105, 109
analog technology: cell phones, 3–5, 36, 56, 104; radios, 18–19, 30, 33; landline telephones, 18, 44, 96; Polaroid cameras, 96; television, 14–15, 27, 30, 32, 44, 51, 53, 67, 88, 93, 96, 98; VCRs, 11, 44, 92–93, 96–97, 106
Aokigahara forest, 5, 11, 17, 21–22, 36, 71–90
authenticity, 51, 54, 57–58, 60, 67, 71–72, 80, 82, 90, 100, 109–10; appearance of, 13, 21, 49–51, 60; aura of, 13, 21, 82. *See also* reality
Azuma, Hiroki, 3, 50, 52

Baudrillard, Jean, 16, 51, 55
Bazin, Andre, 15
Blair Witch Project, The, 56–58
boundaries, 3, 15–17, 27, 30, 45, 60, 77, 98, 108–9
Brown, Steven T., 6–8, 11–12, 23, 58, 93

Candyman, 112
Chun, Wendy Hui Kyong, 14, 17, 24n12, 30, 100, 114
circulation, 3, 5, 7, 9–10, 13, 19–20, 22–46, 51, 53–55, 57, 68, 71–72, 76, 79, 83–86, 88, 98–100, 108–10, 114–15
Cloverfield, 59, 110n2
copying. *See* replication
copy-paste, 26, 31, 36, 47
countryside, 33–36, 112
COVID-19, 22, 90, 111–14
Cure (*Kyua*), 6, 8

data, 9, 14, 19, 107
database consumption, 3, 50, 52–53, 60, 63, 65, 68
Deleuze, Gilles, 9–11
digital: borders, 88, 113; copying, 9, 13, 19, 92, 105–9; images, 19, 22, 23n4, 37–38; interfaces, 3–4, 19–20, 27, 32, 35–38, 40, 92–93, 100–1, 106, 110n1; media technology, 3–4, 15, 18–20, 104–5, 109, 113–14; storytelling, 33, 40, 46; urban legends, 20, 31, 33, 42; world, 13, 34, 36, 109–10. *See also* smartphones
digital media, 3–4, 7, 14–15, 27, 83, 92, 100, 104–9; spectrality of, 9, 27, 32, 36

131

Don't Look Up (Joyūrei), 18, 93, 105
Dumas, Raechel, 10–11, 23, 97

Enchō, 25, 29

Figal, Gerald, 26, 28–29
Forest, The, 21, 72, 84–88, 90n9
Foster, Michael Dylan, 26–28, 33
frames, 15–17, 19, 21–23, 26–28, 37–40, 46, 50, 55–57, 60, 65–68, 72, 79–80, 84–86, 91, 100–3, 106–9, 111, 113, 115; boundaries of, 3, 15–17, 27, 45, 108–9; fractured, 5, 16–17, 21, 50, 102, 111; frames-within-frames, 5, 7, 40, 44, 67, 78–80, 93, 98, 100; nested, 15–16, 107–9
Friedberg, Anne, 15–17, 21, 27, 46, 50–51, 56, 60, 84, 92, 100, 102–3

Galbraith, Patrick, 51, 53–54, 63
Galloway, Alexander, 13, 16, 37, 46, 79, 92–92, 110n1
gaps, 98, 105, 107–9
Gerow, Aaron, 9–11, 115n1
ghost stories (*kaidan*), 25–26, 30, 33–35, 37, 39, 58–59, 66–67, 74, 76
Glico, 54, 58
glow, 96, 101–2
Gray, Jonathan, 23n5
Grudge, The (Ju-on), 2, 6, 9, 23, 59

haunted media, 15, 19, 25, 34, 45, 50, 75, 87, 88, 95
Hayami, Akari, 62–65
horror film, 21, 58–60, 63, 67, 68n4, 114; found-footage, 15, 21, 32, 42, 58–59, 94. *See also* J-horror

idol culture: appearance of realness in, 21, 49–50, 58–60, 63; mutual agreement (*o-yakusoku*), 21, 50–51, 54, 56, 58, 67; performativity in, 50–51, 53–54, 59–63, 65–67
infection, 10, 22, 34, 95, 98, 103, 105
Instagram, 2–3, 17, 34, 91–92

interfaces, 15–16, 26, 37, 40, 92–93, 106, 110n1
Internet, 3, 6, 9, 11, 19–20, 24, 26–27, 30–38, 45, 47, 49, 53, 56, 77–78, 85, 101, 103–4, 115
intimacy, 9, 14, 21, 30–31, 78, 80, 82–84
Ishii, Teruyoshi, 18, 50, 59
isolation, 8–9, 31, 87, 111
Itō, Ryūhei, 31–33
Ivy, Marilyn, 81

Japan: exoticization of, 80–84, 88; social problems, 8, 11; suicide in, 9, 11, 73–75, 81, 83, 89n4, 90n5; urban-rural divide, 26, 28, 33, 36, 41
J-horror, 4, 6–8, 10–11, 20, 23, 32, 36, 44, 58–60, 75, 93–94, 97–98, 105, 109

Kadokawa Corporation, 12, 99–100
Karlin, Jason G., 51, 53–54, 63
Kinoshita, Chika, 4, 6, 23, 44, 59–60, 93–94, 97–98, 105
Koma, Natsumi, 2, 91–92
Komatsu, Kazuhiko, 28
Konaka, Chiaki, 6, 44, 58, 93, 96–97, 113
kuchi-sake-onna (slit-mouthed woman), 26, 28, 33, 40, 59
Kurosawa, Kiyoshi, 3, 6, 8–9, 12, 23, 61

Laird, Colleen, 68n1, 94, 98, 105
LINE, 1, 91
live scare experiences, 112–14
live video broadcasting, 3, 17, 19, 76–77, 100–2, 113
looking, 35, 37–39, 65, 108; clickbait as, 35

Maekawa, Osamu, 3–4, 7, 10–11, 23n6, 47n4, 98
manga, 2, 8, 12, 20, 22, 46, 73, 99, 101, 105, 109
Manovich, Lev, 3, 14, 23n4, 24n12, 26, 89

materiality, 4, 9, 13, 18–19, 32, 75, 94–95, 105, 109
media anxiety, 2, 13, 20, 97, 104, 115
media mix, 99
mediation, 21, 37, 44, 82, 95, 97; multiple layers of, 16, 38, 42, 67, 113. *See also* remediation
memes, 11, 109
Memoirs of a Geisha (novel), 82
Minegishi, Minami, 51, 57
Miyazaki, Tsutomu, 8
Momoiro Clover Z, 49, 52, 61–66, 68–69
music videos, 61, 71, 89, 91
mutation, 97, 99–100, 109
MX4D technology, 21, 77–78, 80

Nakata, Hideo, 1, 6, 8, 12, 18, 22, 24, 59–60, 92–97, 99, 104, 107
narratives, 5–6, 18, 35, 46, 56, 76, 91–92, 97, 111, 113–14; film, 7, 15–17, 21, 27, 41, 50, 60, 66, 79–80, 98–102, 108; grand, 3, 52–53, 55, 68; horror, 3–7, 10, 19–20, 22–23, 30, 34, 40, 44–45, 58, 67, 71, 77, 88, 109, 112–14; Orientalist, 11, 84, 87; small, 3, 52–53, 55, 68
2channel, 17, 20–21, 25–40, 46, 47n8, 49, 67, 76, 101, 103
2channel Curse (*2channeru no noroi*), 20, 27, 32, 35–38, 46, 49, 103
new media, 3, 5, 7, 10–11, 13–24, 26–28, 30, 32, 40, 42–46, 72, 77–78, 80, 88, 92, 100, 104, 107, 109, 114–15
Niconico, 3, 17, 19, 21, 26, 42–43, 45–46, 49, 80, 92–93, 99–101, 103–4, 106, 109; scrolling comments on, 42–43, 101
nihonjinron, 83, 90
noroi no dōga (cursed video), 20, 27, 36, 59, 104
nostalgia, 7, 26–27, 41, 45

obasute (abandoning the elderly), 76, 83

Odaiba Joypolis amusement park, 5, 114
offscreen space, 15. *See also* frames
old media, 14, 20, 26–27, 45, 92, 115
One Cut of the Dead (*Kamera wo tomeru na!*), 111–12
One Cut of the Dead: Mission: Remote (*Kamera wo tomeru na! Rimōto daisakusen*), 111–12
One Missed Call (*Chakushin ari*), 2, 8–9, 12
Orientalism, 80–84, 88
otaku, 2, 8, 46, 52
Ōtsuka, Eiji, 52

pandemic, 22–23, 111–14. *See also* COVID-19
paratexts, 3, 5, 20, 23n5, 28, 37–38, 46, 79–80, 92, 96; marketing, 1, 3, 5, 12, 17, 27–28, 42, 45, 56, 63, 77, 92, 100, 108; publicity stunts, 20, 22, 91–92, 108
parody, 92, 99, 109, 111
photography, 4, 18, 50, 61, 94
Pokemon Go, 74, 89
pop-up windows, 35, 94, 103
Psychic Vision (*Jaganrei*), 18, 21, 32, 50, 59–63, 94–95, 97, 105
Pulse (*Kairo*), 3, 6, 8–9, 11–13, 19, 45

rakugo, 25, 29–30
reality, 11, 13, 15–16, 19–21, 24n11, 29, 36, 44, 49, 51, 54–60, 66–67, 75–78, 80, 82, 87–88, 100; fiction and, 9, 30, 49, 62, 64; fractured, 5, 9, 11, 13, 17, 20–22, 32, 40, 49–68, 72, 102, 109–10, 111, 115; mediated, 4, 15–16, 51, 55, 100, 113. *See also* authenticity
red room curse, 35–36, 103
reflection, 3, 16, 37, 39, 93, 95, 100–2, 106–7
remediation, 5, 9. *See also* mediation
replication, 3, 9, 99. *See also* digital, copying

Ring (*Ringu*), 3–4, 6, 8–13, 18, 22–23, 35, 40, 44–45, 47, 59–60; franchise, 1, 4, 22, 42, 78, 91–110
Rings, 22, 91–92, 99, 107–9
Ring Virus, The, 91, 98

Sadako, 1, 22, 92–93, 99, 104–9, 111n5
Sadako (character), 1–5, 9–11, 18, 22, 35, 40, 91–93, 95–97, 99–100, 103–10, 111n5, 116–17
Sadako at the End of the World (*Shūmatsu no Sadako-san*), 3, 91
Sadako-san and Sadako-chan (*Sadako-san to Sadako-chan*), 99, 105
Sadako 3D, 19, 22, 43, 77, 93, 99–104, 106–9, 111n5
Sadako 3D 2, 99, 111n5
Sadako vs. Kayako, 2, 59, 92, 106–7
Samejima Incident, The (*Samejima jiken*), 36, 113
Sanyūtei Enchō. *See* Enchō
Sconce, Jeffrey, 15, 18–19, 97
screens, 3–5, 11, 15–23, 26–28, 38–39, 51, 55–56, 65, 67–68, 72, 79, 88, 91–92, 98, 100–4, 106, 108–13, 115. *See also* interfaces
shifting perspective, 17, 21, 43–44, 46, 65–67, 72, 78, 80, 88, 95, 102
Shimizu, Takashi, 6, 9, 12–13, 72, 75, 79
shinrei shashin (spirit photography), 18, 50, 61, 106
Shiraishi, Kōji, 2, 13, 40, 49, 57, 59, 62–66, 92
smartphones, 1, 3, 7, 18, 20–22, 26–27, 32, 36–38, 42–43, 45–46, 93, 104–6, 110n5, 111–12
social media, 1, 3–5, 7, 9, 11, 16–20, 22, 34–35, 59–60, 92, 105, 109, 113–15
spectacle, 16–17, 52, 55, 60, 67, 72, 99, 112
spectrality, 18–20, 27–28, 32, 50, 61, 72, 88, 94, 106, 113

Steinberg, Marc, 13, 31, 42
Suicide Forest Village (*Jukai mura*), 6, 12–13, 17, 21, 72, 75–80, 84, 88, 100, 102
Suzuki, Kōji, 91, 99, 107, 110n6, 111

Takahashi, Hiroshi, 6–9, 23, 27, 41, 43–44, 47, 61, 73, 94–97, 113
talent (*tarento*), 12, 53, 68n3
tangibility. *See* materiality
Thinkmodo, 108
Toshimaen (theme park), 17, 41–42
Toshimaen: The Movie (*Eiga: Toshimaen*), 9, 13, 17, 20, 23, 25, 27, 40–47, 49, 76–78, 94, 100, 104
Train Man (*Densha otoko*), 31, 46
True Scary Stories (*Hontō ni atta kowai hanashi*), 8, 58, 93–94
Twitter, 3, 5, 17, 34, 112, 115

urban legends, 17, 20, 26–27, 42, 47n4, 47n7–8, 49, 59, 62, 75, 77, 93

video streaming, 3–5, 7, 18–19, 23, 26, 36, 42, 46, 66–67, 92–93, 100, 104, 106, 112, 115, 115n2
virtual idols, 54–55
virtual windows, 13–20, 22, 85, 91–92, 99–103, 111

Wada-Marciano, Mitsuyo, 4, 6–7, 9, 32, 98–104

yōkai (folk monsters), 26, 28–29
Yomota, Inuhiko, 7
YouTube, 3, 5, 17, 20–21, 26, 43, 49, 60, 71–72, 74, 76–80, 83–84, 88–90, 92, 104–6, 109
yūrei (ghost), 85, 87

Zahlten, Alexander, 8, 12–13, 58, 93, 99
Zenshōan Temple, 25–26
Zoom, 22, 111–12, 115, 116n3

About the Author

Lindsay Nelson is an assistant professor in the Department of Political Science and Economics at Meiji University, where she teaches English, Japanese popular culture, and Japanese cinema. Her work has appeared in *East Asian Journal of Popular Culture*, *Journal of Japanese and Korean Cinema*, and *Japanese Studies*.

www.ingramcontent.com/pod-product-compliance
Lightning Source LLC
Chambersburg PA
CBHW061718300426
44115CB00014B/2744